WOO

MOVIE ★ ICONS

KELLY

EDITOR
PAUL DUNCAN

TEXT
GLENN HOPP

PHOTOS
THE KOBAL COLLECTION

TASCHEN

HONG KONG KÖLN LONDON LOS ANGELES MADRID PARIS TOKYO

CONTENTS

1

GRACE KELLY: COOL BEAUTY

BY GLENN HOPP

GRACE KELLY: KÜHLE SCHÖNHEIT

GRACE KELLY : BEAUTÉ FROIDE

GRACE KELLY: COOL BEAUTY

by Glenn Hopp

Rear Window probably best reveals Grace Kelly's status as a movie icon. The film is often called Alfred Hitchcock's "testament film," meaning that in style and content it offers a representative summation of his career. But the movie could also be considered as Kelly's testament film because it epitomizes the qualities that made her an enduring public icon.

At the same time that Kelly was offered the female lead in *Rear Window*, she was also offered the part opposite Marlon Brando in *On the Waterfront* (a character eventually played by Eva Marie Saint). Both were great roles, and Grace understandably stalled her agent Jay Kanter while she considered her options. Her tone in describing this key moment decades later to Hitchcock biographer Donald Spoto suggests that she savored being in such an enviable, in-demand position. And rightly so. In front of her in those two masterful scripts, she had proof that she had arrived.

She chose the movie star role rather than the acting part, which is not to say that essentially playing herself in the part of Lisa Fremont was easy. Cary Grant told biographer James Spada that being yourself "is the toughest thing to do if you're an actor, because if you're yourself, the audience feels as though that person is living and breathing, just being natural, not 'acting.'" Lisa Fremont represents Grace's essential iconic traits: cool beauty, depths of hidden passion, intelligence, playfulness, style – in short, the qualities that led James Spada to say that "in some ways Grace Kelly was 'the pious man's Marilyn.'"

Rear Window, made in 1954 – the year Grace was the top female box-office star - fell out of distribution from 1968 until 1983. Most audiences in 1983 would have been seeing the film for the first time and may even have been unaware of its premise of L. B. Jeffries, the wheelchair-bound photographer, wondering if the neighbor he has been idly observing has murdered his wife. When the disapproving, skeptical Lisa sees that Lars Thorwald (Raymond Burr), the

PORTRAIT (1952)

"She will probably go through life being completely misunderstood, since she usually says completely what she means."
Cary Grant, actor

neighbor about whom James Stewart harbors dark suspicions, has suddenly packed his belongings to decamp from his apartment, she becomes curious. Hitchcock's camera emphasizes the moment by moving in slowly on Grace's beautiful, worried face: "Let's start again from the beginning, Jeff. Tell me what you saw, and what ... you think ... it means." It's a truly thrilling moment when a movie shifts gears and takes its viewers off on a long, suspenseful ride. Many audiences in 1983 are said to have applauded at that scene. Even after twenty-nine years, the power of the testament film had not dimmed.

Grace made ten other films in only three and one-half years during her Hollywood career before marrying Prince Rainier of Monaco in 1956 and retiring from the screen. Most of her roles are strengthened by the tension between the classy, calm surface and the contrasting emotions beneath. This tension seems not to have been limited to cinematic parts alone. In 1975, for example, Grace sat looking at a different kind of manuscript, an unpublished biography about her. The author, Gwen Robyns, had managed to assemble the mostly unknown accounts of Grace's Hollywood romances. Princess Grace met with Robyns in Paris in a friendly, private conversation that took them both through the manuscript fact by awkward fact. Grace confirmed it all, and then asked the author to delete it all: "How can I bring up my daughters not to have an affair with a married man when I was having affairs with married men all the time?" She revealed a genuine vulnerability mixed with a frankness that appealed to Robyns: "All right. Everything comes out."

Robyns was taken into Grace's inner circle as a friendship developed. Years after the tragic death of Princess Grace, the fullness of Grace Kelly's love life was supplied by subsequent writers and often in a tawdry rather than a realistic way. "I was crazy," Robyns later told biographer Robert Lacey. "But that is just not my style. She'd told me about her daughters ... what would have happened to her, personally, if I had published it? I just couldn't do that to her." Robyns had been won over. Even after two decades, the power of the icon had not dimmed.

GRACE KELLY: KÜHLE SCHÖNHEIT

von Glenn Hopp

Grace Kellys Status als Filmikone wird wahrscheinlich am deutlichsten, wenn man sie sich in *Rear Window (Das Fenster zum Hof)* anschaut. Dieser Film gilt vielen als cineastisches Vermächtnis Alfred Hitchcocks, der Stil und Inhalt seines Lebenswerks repräsentiert und zusammenfasst. Genauso kann man ihn auch als Grace Kellys Vermächtnis verstehen, denn er bringt all die Qualitäten auf den Punkt, die sie in den Augen der Öffentlichkeit zu einer Ikone werden ließen.

Als man ihr die weibliche Hauptrolle in *Das Fenster zum Hof* antrug, bot man ihr zeitgleich den Part an der Seite von Marlon Brando in *On the Waterfront (Die Faust im Nacken)* an, den schließlich Eva Marie Saint spielte. Beide Rollen waren großartig, und es war verständlich, dass Grace beide Möglichkeiten erwog und ihren Agenten Jay Kanter eine Weile hinhielt. Die Art, wie sie diesen Schlüsselmoment Jahrzehnte später dem Hitchcock-Biografen Donald Spoto beschreibt, vermittelt, wie sehr sie ihre beneidenswerte Lage genoss, so begehrt zu sein. Mit Recht: Diese beiden hervorragenden Drehbücher waren der endgültige Beweis, dass sie es geschafft hatte.

Sie gab der Rolle des Filmstars den Vorzug vor der schauspielerischen Herausforderung, was nicht bedeuten sollte, dass ihr leichtfiel, in der Rolle der Lisa Fremont im Grunde sich selbst zu spielen. Cary Grant erzählte dem Biografen James Spada, sich selbst darzustellen „[ist] das Schwierigste für einen Schauspieler. Wenn du du selbst bist, hat das Publikum den Eindruck, dass diese Person lebt und atmet und sich so gibt, wie sie ist, ohne zu ‚schauspielern‘". Lisa Fremont verkörpert die wesentlichen Eigenschaften der Ikone Grace Kelly: kühle Schönheit, verborgene Leidenschaft, Intelligenz, Verspieltheit und Stil – kurzum: jene Züge, die James Spada zu der Aussage veranlassten, Grace Kelly „sei in gewisser Weise die ‚Marilyn des frommen Mannes‘ gewesen".

PORTRAIT FOR 'HIGH NOON' (1952)

„Vermutlich wird sie ihr ganzes Leben lang völlig missverstanden werden, weil sie normalerweise immer genau das sagt, was sie meint."
Cary Grant, Schauspieler

Das Fenster zum Hof entstand 1954 – in dem Jahr, in dem Grace die Nummer 1 unter den weiblichen Kinostars war –, war allerdings von 1968 bis 1983 nicht im Vertrieb. Wahrscheinlich haben die meisten Zuschauer den Film im Jahr 1983 zum ersten Mal gesehen und kannten nicht einmal die Story: Weil er vorübergehend an den Rollstuhl gefesselt ist, beobachtet der Fotograf L. B. „Jeff" Jefferies aus Langeweile seinen Nachbarn Lars Thorwald (Raymond Burr) mit dem Fernglas, und in ihm keimt der Verdacht, dass dieser seine Frau ermordet hat. Lisa ist zunächst skeptisch und missbilligt Jeffs Voyeurismus, wird aber neugierig, als Thorwald seine Siebensachen packt, um aus seiner Wohnung auszuziehen. Hitchcock betont diesen Augenblick des Sinneswandels, indem er mit der Kamera langsam auf Graces hübsches, sorgenvolles Gesicht zufährt: „Fangen wir wieder ganz von vorn an, Jeff: Sag mir alles, was du gesehen hast … und meinst, … was es bedeutet." In diesem spannungsgeladenen Augenblick ändert der Film schlagartig sein Tempo, und für das Publikum beginnt eine lange, nervenaufreibende Achterbahnfahrt. Es wird berichtet, dass 1983 viele Zuschauer an dieser Stelle applaudiert hätten: Selbst 29 Jahre nach seiner Entstehung hatte das Vermächtnis nichts von seiner Faszination verloren.

In ihrer nur dreieinhalb Jahre währenden Hollywoodkarriere drehte Grace zehn weitere Filme, bevor sie 1956 Fürst Rainier von Monaco heiratete und sich aus dem Filmgeschäft zurückzog. Die meisten ihrer Rollen gewinnen an Tiefe durch die Spannung zwischen ihrem vornehm-gelassenen Äußeren und den unter der Oberfläche brodelnden, gegenteiligen Gefühlen – und diese Spannung scheint sich nicht auf ihre Filmrollen beschränkt zu haben. 1975 las Gracia Patricia beispielsweise eine andere Art von Manuskript, nämlich eine unveröffentlichte Biografie über ihre Person. Der Autorin, Gwen Robyns, war es gelungen, die weitgehend unbekannten Hollywoodromanzen der Fürstin zusammenzutragen. Die beiden Frauen trafen sich anschließend in Paris zu einem freundlichen privaten Gespräch, in dessen Verlauf sie das Manuskript Peinlichkeit für Peinlichkeit durchgingen. Fürstin Gracia bestätigte alles und bat die Biografin dann, es zu streichen: „Wie soll ich meine Töchter dazu erziehen, keine Affären mit verheirateten Männern anzufangen, wenn ich selbst ständig solche Affären hatte?" Damit zeigte sie nicht nur, wie verwundbar sie war, sondern bewies auch eine Offenheit, die Robyns beeindruckte: „In Ordnung. Es wird alles gestrichen."

Die aus diesem Gespräch resultierende Freundschaft verschaffte Robyns schließlich Zugang zum inneren Kreis um die Fürstin. Jahre nach deren tragischem Unfalltod schilderten andere Autoren ausführlich Grace Kellys Liebesleben, oftmals eher reißerisch als realistisch. „Ich war verrückt", erzählte Robyns später dem Biografen Robert Lacey, „aber das ist einfach nicht mein Stil. Sie hatte mir von ihren Töchtern erzählt … Was wäre mit ihr persönlich passiert, wenn ich alles veröffentlicht hätte? Das konnte ich ihr nicht antun." Grace Kelly hatte damals Robyns für sich gewonnen. Selbst nach zwei Jahrzehnten hatte die Ikone nichts von ihrer Kraft eingebüßt.

PORTRAIT (1955)

GRACE KELLY : BEAUTÉ FROIDE

Glenn Hopp

C'est probablement *Fenêtre sur cour* qui a définitivement élevé Grace Kelly au rang d'icône du 7ᵉ art. Ce « film testament » d'Alfred Hitchcock - comme on l'a souvent appelé - offre par son style et son contenu un résumé fidèle de la carrière du maître du suspense. Mais il pourrait également être considéré comme le film testament de Grace Kelly, tant il est l'illustration parfaite des qualités qui ont fait de l'actrice une idole adulée du public.

Lorsqu'on lui propose le premier rôle féminin dans *Fenêtre sur cour*, elle se voit en même temps proposée de donner la réplique à Marlon Brando dans *Sur les quais* (un rôle finalement attribué à Eva Marie Saint). Comme on peut le comprendre, Grace hésite entre les deux rôles, aussi importants à ses yeux l'un et l'autre, et laisse son agent Jay Kanter dans l'expectative. Lorsque, quelques dizaines d'années plus tard, elle évoquera avec Donald Spoto, le biographe de Hitchcock, ce moment charnière de sa carrière, elle ne laissera aucun doute sur le sentiment de fierté procuré par tant de sollicitations. Et pour cause ! Face à ces deux scénarios de premier plan, elle avait pu mesurer toute l'ampleur de sa nouvelle notoriété.

Son choix se porte alors sur le rôle de star - au détriment du rôle de composition -, ce qui ne veut pas dire que jouer son propre rôle sous les traits de Lisa Fremont est chose facile. Comme le reconnaîtra Cary Grant à son biographe James Spada, jouer son propre rôle « est la chose la plus difficile qui soit pour un acteur, parce que lorsque vous incarnez votre propre personnage, les spectateurs vous voient comme un être en chair et en os, et non comme un acteur ». Le personnage de Lisa Fremont incarne parfaitement les traits essentiels de Grace : beauté froide, passion profonde, intelligence, fantaisie, style - en un mot, toutes les qualités qui font dire à James Spada que « par certains côtés, Grace incarne la "Marilyn de l'homme bleu" ».

Tourné en 1954, l'année où Grace est au sommet du box-office, *Fenêtre sur cour* est retiré de la distribution en 1968. Lorsqu'il est rejoué en 1983, la plupart des spectateurs le découvrent

PORTRAIT (1952)

> « *Elle restera incomprise probablement toute sa vie, puisqu'elle a l'habitude de dire tout ce qu'elle pense.* »
> Cary Grant, acteur

pour la première fois, ignorant probablement tout de la trame du film : L. B. Jeffries (« Jeff »), un photographe cloué dans un fauteuil roulant, soupçonne le voisin qu'il observe passivement depuis sa fenêtre d'avoir assassiné sa femme. Lorsque Lisa, sceptique et critique envers l'attitude de Jeff, constate que Lars Thorwald (Raymond Burr), le voisin à propos duquel James Stewart nourrit de sombres soupçons, quitte précipitamment son appartement après l'avoir vidé de ses effets personnels, sa curiosité est piquée à vif. La caméra de Hitchcock souligne ce moment clé par un lent travelling avant sur le visage tourmenté de Grace : « Recommençons depuis le début, Jeff. Dites-moi tout ce que vous avez vu … et aussi … ce que vous en pensez. » L'atmosphère chargée de tension annonce un changement de rythme qui va entraîner les spectateurs dans une longue et palpitante intrigue riche en rebondissements. Dans les salles obscures, de nombreux spectateurs auraient même applaudi. Vingt-neuf ans après sa première sortie, la puissance de ce film testament est toujours intacte.

Avant d'épouser le prince Rainier en 1956, mettant ainsi un terme à sa carrière hollywoodienne, Grace tournera dix autres films en l'espace d'à peine trois ans et demi. La plupart des personnages qu'elle incarne à l'écran prennent de l'épaisseur, une épaisseur nourrie par une tension permanente entre une image extérieure sereine et raffinée, et des émotions intérieures tout en contrastes. Cette tension ne se limite pas, semble-t-il, à ses rôles cinématographiques. C'est ainsi, par exemple, qu'en 1975 Grace tient entre ses mains un « scénario » d'un autre genre : sa propre biographie. Son auteur, Gwen Robyns, est parvenu à rassembler les chroniques des idylles hollywoodiennes de l'actrice, pour la plupart restées secrètes. La princesse Grace et Robyns se rencontrent à Paris pour un entretien privé et amical où chaque passage délicat et embarrassant du manuscrit est passé au crible. Grace confirme chaque détail avant de demander à l'auteur de tout supprimer, se justifiant ainsi : « Comment pourrais-je élever mes filles dans l'idée qu'elles ne doivent pas avoir d'aventures avec des hommes mariés alors que moi-même, je les ai multipliées. » Sa réelle vulnérabilité mêlée de franchise achève de convaincre Robyns, qui accède à sa demande : « Très bien, on retire tout. »

Au fil de leur amitié grandissante, Robyns est accueilli dans le cercle intime de Grace. Des années après la mort tragique de la princesse, tous les détails de la vie amoureuse de Grace Kelly seront dévoilés sous la plume d'une succession d'écrivains dans un style plus proche du sensationnalisme que du réalisme. « J'étais furieux », confiera plus tard Robyns au biographe Robert Lacey. « Ce n'est pas du tout mon style. Elle m'avait parlé de ses filles … Quelles auraient été les conséquences pour Grace si j'avais publié tous ces détails ? Je n'aurais jamais pu lui faire une chose pareille. » Deux décennies après sa disparition, Robyns était toujours sous le charme de la princesse. L'icône n'avait rien perdu de son aura.

2

VISUAL FILMOGRAPHY

FILMOGRAFIE IN BILDERN

FILMOGRAPHIE EN IMAGES

STILL FROM 'HIGH NOON' (1952)
Grace on Gary Cooper's acting: "You look into his face
and see everything he is thinking." / Grace über Gary
Coopers Schauspielkunst: „Du schaust ihm ins Gesicht
und siehst alles, was er denkt." / Grace Kelly à propos
du jeu d'acteur de Gary Cooper: « Il suffit de le
regarder en face pour lire dans ses pensées. »

PAGES 26/27
STILL FROM 'HIGH NOON' (1952)
Gary Cooper, Grace, and Katy Jurado. / Gary Cooper,
Grace und Katy Jurado. / Gary Cooper, Grace Kelly et
Katy Jurado.

PORTRAIT FOR 'HIGH NOON' (1952)
Grace Kelly as Amy Fowler Kane, the Quaker bride. /
Grace Kelly als Quäkerbraut Amy Fowler Kane. / Grace
Kelly dans le rôle d'Amy Fowler Kane, la jeune épouse
quaker.

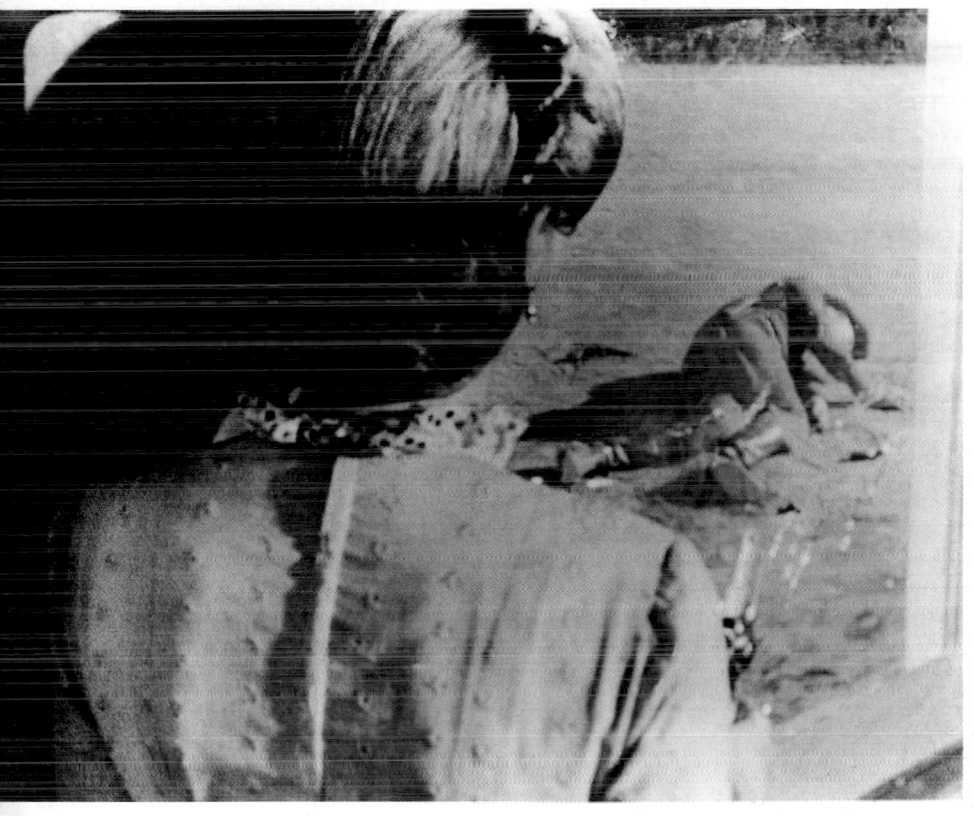

STILL FROM 'HIGH NOON' (1952)
Director Fred Zinnemann uses a shot from Amy's
point of view to convey her feelings of guilt. / In dieser
Einstellung aus Amys Blickwinkel vermittelt Regisseur
Fred Zinnemann ihre Schuldgefuhle. / La caméra
subjective du réalisateur Fred Zinnemann suggère
avec habileté le sentiment de culpabilité d'Amy.

STILL FROM 'HIGH NOON' (1952)
Amy conquers her pacifism, killing one of her husband's
foes. / Amy überwindet ihren Pazifismus und tötet
einen der Feinde ihres Ehemanns. / Bien qu'adepte de
la non-violence, Amy surmonte ses réticences et abat
l'un des ennemis de son mari.

" ALRIGHT. DOANE COME ON OUT — ETC

STORYBOARD FOR 'HIGH NOON' (1952)
The sketch centers on the villain using Amy as a
shield ... / Die Skizze konzentriert sich auf den
Bösewicht, der Amy als Schutzschild benutzt ... / Cet
extrait du story-board se focalise sur la froideur du
bandit sans foi ni loi qui retient Amy comme bouclier
humain ...

"Audrey [Hepburn] had enormous self-confidence
while Grace, so far as I could see, was not self-
confident at all. Certainly not at this stage. She
was her own problem, so to speak. Instead of
looking out at the world, she was looking inward,
into herself, a great deal."
Fred Zinnemann, director

„Audrey [Hepburn] war sehr selbstbewusst,
während Grace, soweit ich es beurteilen kann,
überhaupt kein Selbstbewusstsein besaß, jedenfalls
nicht zu diesem Zeitpunkt. Sie stand sich
sozusagen selbst im Wege. Statt hinaus in die Welt
zu schauen, blickte sie sehr oft nach innen, in sich
selbst hinein."
Fred Zinnemann, Regisseur

STILL FROM 'HIGH NOON' (1952)
... whilst the finished shot better conveys Cooper's point of view and mixed emotions. / ... während die endgültige Einstellung besser Wills (Coopers) Sicht entspricht und seine gemischten Gefühle vermittelt. / ... tandis que le plan final révèle le point de vue et les émotions mêlées de Will (Gary Cooper).

PAGES 32/33
STILL FROM 'HIGH NOON' (1952)
The final shootout (Ian McDonald, Grace, Gary Cooper). / Der letzte Schusswechsel (Ian McDonald, Grace, Gary Cooper). / La fusillade finale (Ian McDonald, Grace Kelly et Gary Cooper).

« Audrey [Hepburn] avait une assurance hors du commun, tandis que Grace, pour autant que j'aie pu m'en rendre compte, manquait cruellement de confiance en soi – en tout cas à cette époque-là. Elle portait pour ainsi dire en elle-même ses propres problèmes. Au lieu de s'ouvrir sur le monde extérieur, elle se complaisait dans l'introspection. »
Fred Zinnemann, réalisateur

STILL FROM 'HIGH NOON' (1952)
The marshall resigns. Floyd Crosby won a Golden Globe
for his cinematography. / Der Marshall legt sein Amt
nieder. Floyd Crosby erhielt einen Golden Globe für
seine Kameraarbeit. / Le marshal démissionne. *Le train
sifflera trois fois* vaudra à Floyd Crosby le Golden Globe
de la Meilleure photographie.

STILL FROM 'HIGH NOON' (1952)
Husband and wife reunited after the violence. /
Nach dem Blutbad sind Mann und Frau wieder vereint. /
Les époux réunis après le bain de sang.

STILL FROM 'MOGAMBO' (1953)
Grace in Africa for location shooting with Donald
Sinden and Ava Gardner. / Grace in Afrika bei den
Dreharbeiten mit Donald Sinden und Ava Gardner. /
Tournage en décors naturels en Afrique. Grace Kelly est
aux côtés de Donald Sinden et d'Ava Gardner.

STILL FROM 'MOGAMBO' (1953)
Grace and Ava Gardner became life-long friends after
working together. / Nach den Dreharbeiten wurden
Grace und Ava Gardner Freundinnen fürs Leben. /
La collaboration de Grace Kelly et Ava Gardner à
l'écran s'est soldée par une longue et solide amitié dans
la vraie vie.

STILL FROM 'MOGAMBO' (1953)
The ensemble cast was directed by John Ford (not pictured). / Das Schauspielerensemble spielte unter der Regie von John Ford (nicht im Bild). / La distribution d'ensemble est placée sous la houlette de John Ford (non visible sur la photo).

PAGES 40/41
STILL FROM 'MOGAMBO' (1953)
Ava Gardner wrote in her autobiography: 'And Donald Sinden, he was so much in love with Gracie. Oh, my God.' / Ava Gardner schrieb in ihrer Autobiografie: „Und Donald Sinden, er war so in Gracie verliebt! O, mein Gott!" / Ava Gardner, dans son autobiographie : « Et ce Donald Sinden, il était tellement amoureux de Gracie. Oh, mon Dieu. »

STILL FROM 'MOGAMBO' (1953)
Clark Gable played the Hemingwayesque hunter. / Clark Gable spielt einen Großwildjäger à la Ernest Hemingway. / Clark Gable en chasseur « hemingwayesque ».

STILL FROM 'MOGAMBO' (1953)
Grace's character was quiet and repressed, Ava
Gardner's brash and boisterous. / Grace spielt eine
stille und unterdrückte, Ava Gardner eine ausgelassene
und ungestüme Frau. / Grace Kelly était d'un naturel
paisible et effacé ; Ava Gardner, d'un tempérament
fougueux et bouillonnant.

STILL FROM 'MOGAMBO' (1953)
Grace: "If 'Mogambo' had been made in Arizona,
I wouldn't have done it." / Grace: „Wäre *Mogambo* in
Arizona gedreht worden, hätte ich nicht mitgemacht." /
Grace Kelly : « Si *Mogambo* avait été tourné en Arizona,
je ne l'aurais pas fait. »

STILL FROM 'MOGAMBO' (1953)
An affair begins between Linda Nordley and the
hunter/guide played by Gable. / Die Affäre zwischen
Linda Nordley und dem Jäger und Führer, den Gable
spielt, nimmt ihren Lauf. / Naissance d'une liaison entre
Linda Nordley et le chasseur et organisateur de safaris
interprété par Gable.

*"Her public persona was so completely different
than her private self that it was phenomenal. She
was so proper, people thought of her as a nun. But
when we were alone together, she used to dance
naked for me to Hawaiian music."*
Don Richardson

STILL FROM 'MOGAMBO' (1953)

„Ihr Auftreten in der Öffentlichkeit war so grundverschieden von ihrer privaten Persönlichkeit, dass man es schon als Phänomen bezeichnen könnte. Sie gab sich so anständig, dass die Leute sie für eine Nonne hielten, aber wenn wir allein waren, tanzte sie nackt vor mir zu Hawaii Musik."
Don Richardson

« Son personnage public était tellement différent de sa personnalité dans la vie de tous les jours. C'était tout simplement phénoménal. Elle était si rangée que les gens la prenaient presque pour une bonne sœur. Mais lorsque nous étions seuls elle et moi, il lui arrivait de danser nue devant moi sur de la musique hawaïenne. »
Don Richardson

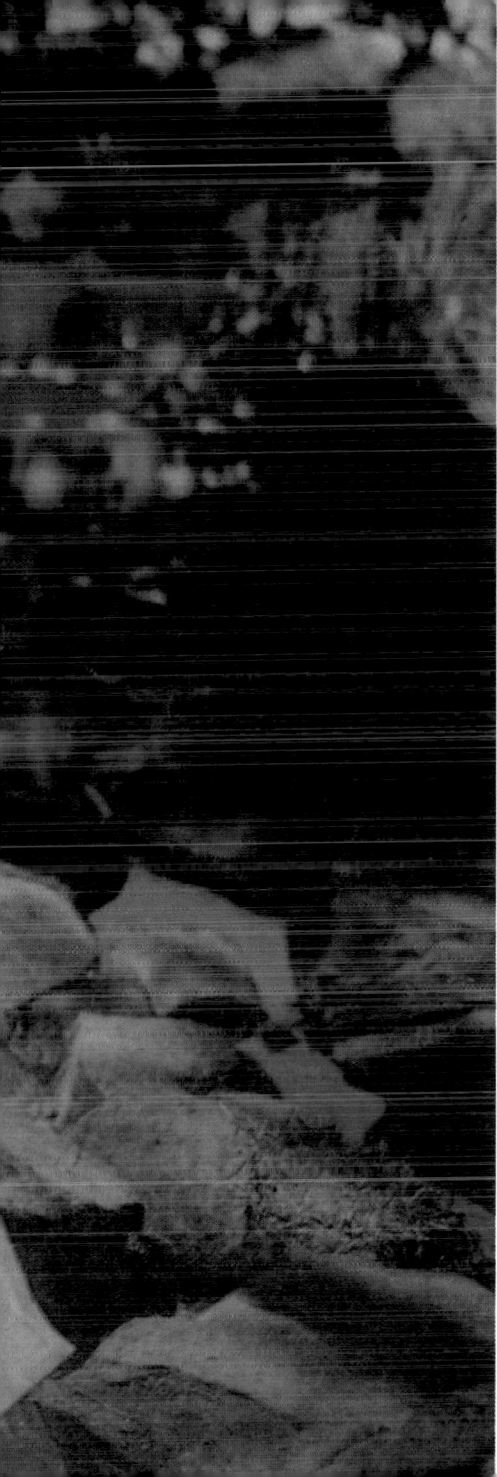

PORTRAIT FOR 'MOGAMBO' (1953)
Grace won a Golden Globe for playing Linda Nordley;
she was also nominated for an Oscar. / Grace erhielt für
ihre Rolle als Linda Nordley einen Golden Globe und
wurde zudem für einen Oscar nominiert. / Nominée
pour un oscar, Grace Kelly a finalement obtenu un
Golden Globe pour son interprétation dans le rôle de
Linda Nordley.

ON THE SET OF 'MOGAMBO' (1953)
Grace snaps pictures on location. / Grace schießt
während der Dreharbeiten ein paar Fotos. / Séance
photos sur les lieux du tournage.

ON THE SET OF 'MOGAMBO' (1953)
Grace and Clark Gable pose with extras on location. /
Grace und Clark Gable posieren am Drehort mit einigen
Komparsen. / Grace Kelly et Clark Gable prennent la
pose avec des figurants sur les lieux du tournage.

PAGES 50/51
STILL FROM 'MOGAMBO' (1953)
Robert Surtees and Freddie Young photographed
'Mogambo.' / Robert Surtees und Freddie Young
standen bei Mogambo hinter der Kamera. / Scène de
Mogambo : la direction de la photographie est signée
Robert Surtees et Freddie Young.

PAGES 52/53
STILL FROM 'MOGAMBO' (1953)
Linda Nordley reaches for a gun when Victor (Gable)
is unfaithful to her. / Als Victor (Gable) sie betrügt,
greift Linda Nordley zum Revolver. / Lorsqu'elle
surprend Victor (Clark Gable) en train de la tromper,
Linda Nordley s'empare d'un revolver.

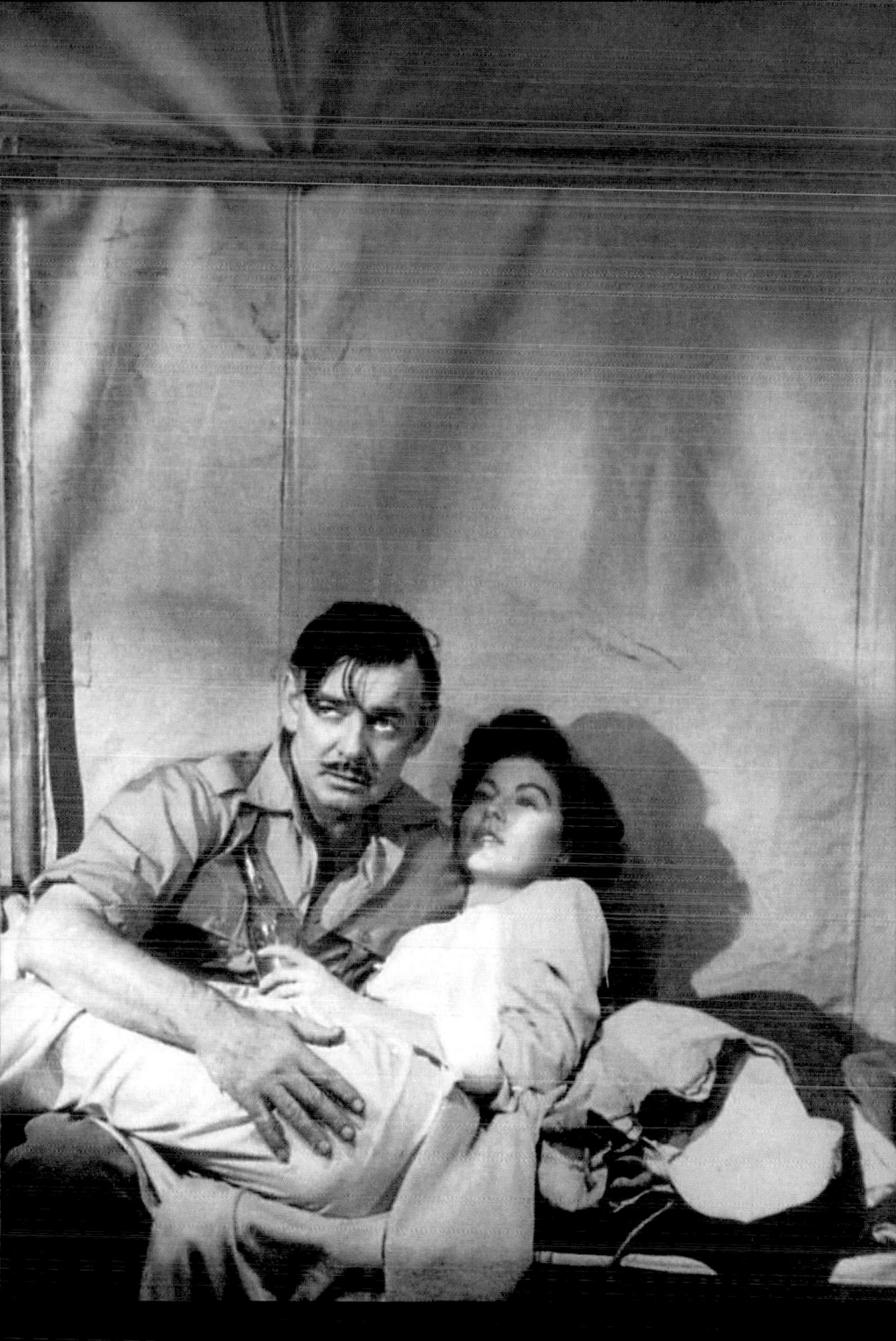

"The subtlety of her sex appeals to me. Grace
conveyed much more sex than the average sexpot.
With Grace, you've got to find it out."
Alfred Hitchcock, director

„Ich finde die subtile Art ihrer Sexualität attraktiv.
Grace brachte viel mehr Erotik rüber als die
durchschnittliche Sexbombe. Bei Grace musste
man es selbst herausfinden."
Alfred Hitchcock, Regisseur

«J'étais attiré par son charme sexuel tout en
subtilité. Grace dégageait plus d'érotisme qu'une
quelconque bombe sexuelle. Mais il fallait le
découvrir par soi-même.»
Alfred Hitchcock, réalisateur

PORTRAIT FOR 'DIAL M FOR MURDER' (1954)
Judy Quine, friend: "Grace made the actual young
woman of the 1950s into a vision of glamour." / Judy
Quine, eine Freundin: „Grace verlieh der realen jungen
Frau aus der Wirklichkeit der 1950er-Jahre etwas
Glamouröses." / Judy Quine, une amie : « Grace a
apporté une note de glamour à l'image de la jeune
femme des années 1950. »

STILL FROM 'DIAL M FOR MURDER' (1954)
Grace suggested to Hitchcock that she wear a
nightgown rather than a robe in the murder scene. /
Grace schlug Hitchcock vor, in der Mordszene ein
Nachthemd anstelle eines Bademantels zu tragen. /
Grace Kelly a suggéré à Hitchcock de porter une robe
de nuit plutôt qu'un peignoir pour la scène du meurtre.

STILL FROM 'DIAL M FOR MURDER' (1954)
The attacker (Anthony Dawson) has been sent by
Margot's husband. / Margots Ehemann hat den
Angreifer (Anthony Dawson) geschickt. / L'agresseur
(Anthony Dawson) a été envoyé par le mari de Margot.

STILL FROM 'DIAL M FOR MURDER' (1954)
François Truffaut: 'Hitchcock filmed scenes of love as if
they were scenes of murder and scenes of murder as if
they were scenes of love.' / François Truffaut:
„Hitchcock drehte Liebesszenen, als ob sie Mordszenen
wären." und Mordszenen, als ob sie Liebesszenen
wären." / François Truffaut : « Alfred Hitchcock filmait
les scènes d'amour comme des scènes de meurtres et
les scènes de meurtres comme des scènes d'amour. »

OPPOSITE/RECHTS/CI-CONTRE
STILL FROM 'DIAL M FOR MURDER' (1954)

PAGES 60/61
STILL FROM 'DIAL M FOR MURDER' (1954)
The husband's murder plan goes awry. / Das
Mordkomplott des Ehemanns geht nicht auf. / Le projet
de meurtre fomenté par le mari tourne court.

STILL FROM 'DIAL M FOR MURDER' (1954)
The shot suggests the emotional distance and wariness
between Tony and Margot. / Die Einstellung suggeriert
die emotionale Kluft und das Misstrauen zwischen Tony
und Margot / La distance émotionnelle et le sentiment
de méfiance entre Tony et Margot sont habilement
suggérés par ce plan.

STILL FROM 'DIAL M FOR MURDER' (1954)
Tony (Ray Milland) returns home and pretends to
comfort his distraught wife. / Tony (Ray Milland) kehrt
nach Hause zurück und gibt vor, seine verzweifelte
Ehefrau zu trösten. / De retour au foyer, Tony (Ray
Milland) feint de réconforter son épouse désemparée.

ON THE SET OF 'DIAL M FOR MURDER' (1954)
Grace on Hitchcock (right): "I have such affection for
him and his wife that he can do no wrong." / Grace
über Hitchcock (rechts): „Ich empfinde eine solche
Zuneigung zu ihm und seiner Frau, dass er nichts falsch
machen kann." / Grace Kelly à propos de Hitchcock
(à droite) : « J'ai tant d'affection pour lui et son épouse ;
je sais que c'est un homme juste. »

STILL FROM 'DIAL M FOR MURDER' (1954)
Robert Cummings plays the lover of Margot Wendice. /
Robert Cummings spielt den Liebhaber von Margot
Wendice. / Robert Cummings joue l'amant de Margot
Wendice.

PAGES 66/67
PORTRAIT (1954)

PAGES 68/69
PORTRAIT FOR 'REAR WINDOW' (1954)
As Lisa Fremont. Andrew Sarris, film historian: "'Rear
Window' is the peak of her career." / Der Filmhistoriker
Andrew Sarris meint: „Das Fenster zum Hof ist der
Höhepunkt ihrer Karriere." / Dans le rôle de Lisa
Fremont. Andrew Sarris, historien du cinéma : « Fenêtre
sur cour représente l'apogée de sa carrière. »

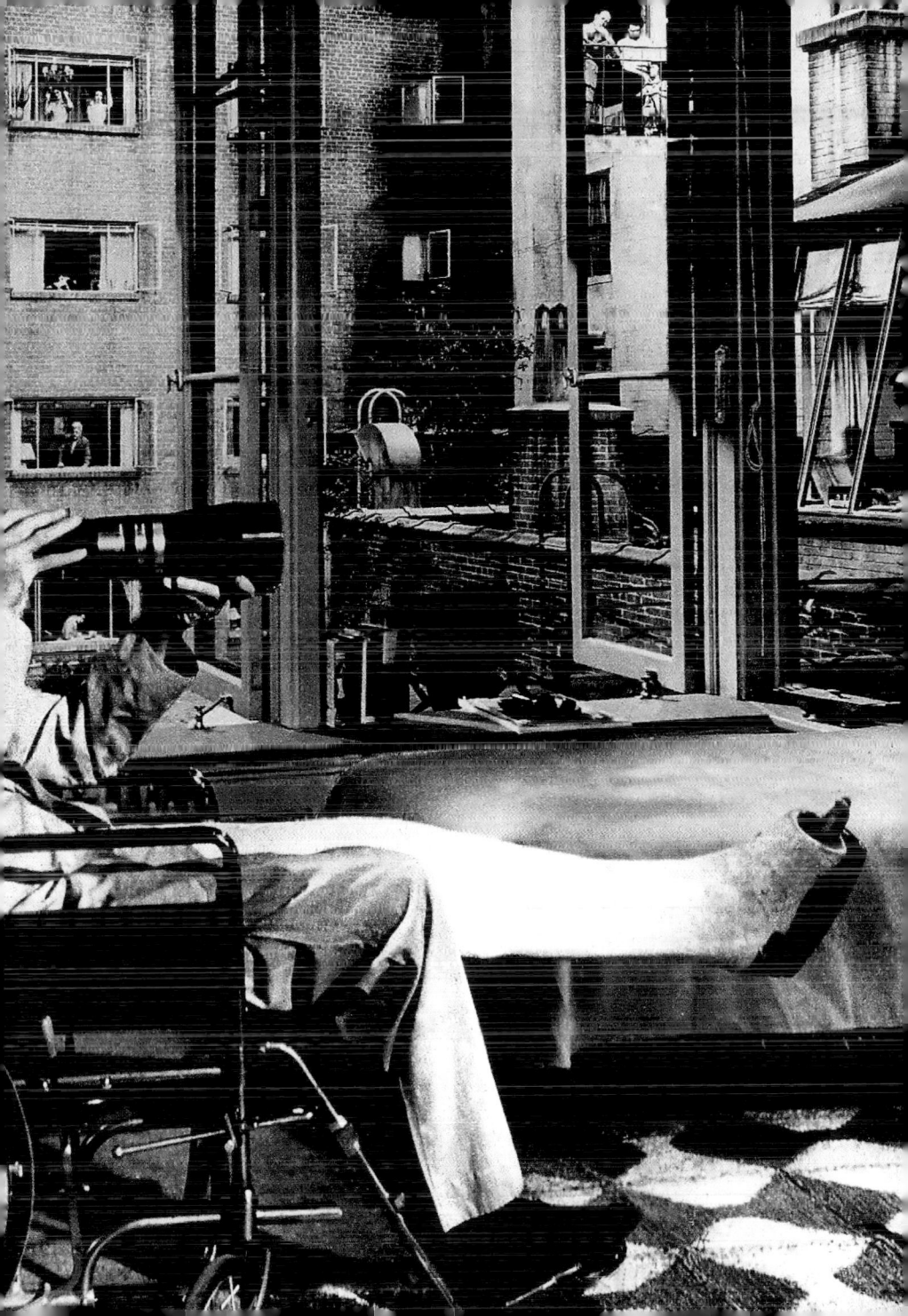

STILL FROM 'REAR WINDOW' (1954)
James Stewart, actor: "Grace has that twinkle and a touch of larceny in her eye." / James Stewart, Schauspieler: „Grace hatte dieses schalkhafte Zwinkern in den Augen." / James Stewart, acteur: « Grace a l'œil pétillant et malicieux. »

STILL FROM 'REAR WINDOW' (1954)
Suspicions of murder must wait while Lisa kisses her wheelchair-bound photographer boyfriend. / Der Mordverdacht muss warten, wenn sie ihren Freund küsst, der im Rollstuhl sitzt. / Scène de baiser avec le photographe cloué dans son fauteuil roulant: les soupçons de meurtre passent momentanément au second plan.

PAGES 74/75
PORTRAIT FOR 'REAR WINDOW' (1954)
Hitchcock biographer Patrick McGilligan: "Hitchcock's camera seemed in love with Kelly." / Hitchcock-Biograf Patrick McGilligan schreibt: „Hitchcocks Kamera schien in Kelly verliebt gewesen zu sein." / Patrick McGilligan, biographe d'Alfred Hitchcock: « Hitchcock tournait comme si sa caméra était amoureuse de Kelly. »

STILL FROM 'REAR WINDOW' (1954)
Wondering about a neighbor's murder whilst spending the night together. / Während sie die Nacht miteinander verbringen, fragen sie sich, ob der Nachbar ein Mörder ist. / Tandis qu'ils passent la nuit ensemble, Lisa et Jeff se demandent si l'appartement d'en face abrite un assassin.

STILL FROM 'REAR WINDOW' (1954)
Lisa Fremont: "Let's start from the beginning again, Jeff. Tell me what you've seen ... and what you think it means." / Lisa Fremont: „Fangen wir wieder ganz von vorn an, Jeff: Sag mir alles, was du gesehen hast ... und meinst, ... was es bedeutet." / Lisa Fremont: « Recommençons depuis le début, Jeff. Dites-moi tout ce que vous avez vu ... et aussi ... ce que vous en pensez. »

ON THE SET OF 'REAR WINDOW' (1954)
Willam Holden visiting the set. Sister Lizanne: "Grace fell in love very easily; too easily, really." / William Holden zu Besuch bei den Dreharbeiten. Grace' Schwester Lizanne: „Grace verliebte sich sehr leicht – tatsächlich zu leicht." / William Holden en visite sur le lieu de tournage. Lizanne, la sœur de Grace Kelly: « Grace tombait facilement amoureuse, vraiment trop facilement. »

PAGES 80/81
STILL FROM 'REAR WINDOW' (1954)
The film's climax with Wendell Corey, Thelma Ritter, Grace, and James Stewart. / Der Höhepunkt des Films, mit Wendell Corey, Thelma Ritter, Grace und James Stewart. / Le point culminant du film avec Wendell Corey, Thelma Ritter, Grace Kelly et James Stewart.

STILL FROM 'REAR WINDOW' (1954)
Lisa sneaks into the flat of Lars Thorwald (Raymond Burr) to find incriminating evidence. / Lisa schleicht sich in die Wohnung von Lars Thorwald (Raymond Burr) auf der Suche nach Beweisen, die ihn überführen könnten. / Lisa s'introduit dans l'appartement de Lars Thorwald (Raymond Burr) à la recherche de pièces à conviction.

STILL FROM 'THE COUNTRY GIRL' (1954)
Flashback: Georgie Elgin (Grace) watches husband
Frank (Bing Crosby, offscreen) at a recording session
before the tragic death of their son. / Rückblende: Vor
dem tragischen Tod ihres Sohnes Johnnie (Jon Provost)
schaut Georgie Elgin (Grace) ihrem Ehemann Frank
(Bing Crosby, außerhalb des Bildes) bei
Plattenaufnahmen zu. / Flash-back: Georgie Elgin
(Grace Kelly) observe Frank (Bing Crosby, hors du
champ de la caméra), son époux, lors d'une séance
d'enregistrement peu de temps avant la mort tragique
de leur fils.

STILL FROM 'THE COUNTRY GIRL' (1954)
Present: Frank is an alcoholic singer/actor frightened of
the role that could make him a star again. / Gegenwart:
Frank ist Sänger, Schauspieler und Alkoholiker, und er
fürchtet sich vor der Rolle, die ihn wieder zum Star
machen könnte. / Retour au présent: en acteur-
chanteur alcoolique, Frank appréhende le rôle qui
pourrait lui rendre son statut de star.

STILL FROM 'THE COUNTRY GIRL' (1954)
Believing that Georgie is the cause of all Frank's problems, Bernie tries to get her out of Frank's life. / Bernie versucht, Georgie aus Franks Leben verschwinden zu lassen, weil er sie für die Ursache aller Übel hält, die Frank plagen. / Convaincu que Georgie est la source de tous les maux qui rongent Frank, Bernie tente de l'écarter de la vie du malheureux.

PAGES 86/87
STILL FROM 'THE COUNTRY GIRL' (1954)
Grace: "I just had to be in 'The Country Girl.' There was a real acting part in it for me." / Grace: „Ich musste einfach in *Ein Mädchen vom Lande* mitspielen. In diesem Film gab es eine echte Charakterrolle für mich." / Grace Kelly : « Il fallait à tout prix que je joue dans *Une fille de province*. Il y avait dans ce film un vrai rôle de composition pour moi. »

STILL FROM 'THE COUNTRY GIRL' (1954)
Bernie Dodd (William Holden) is the director of Frank's comeback vehicle. / Bernie Dodd (William Holden) führt Regie bei dem Film, der Frank zum Comeback verhelfen könnte. / Bernie Dodd (William Holden) est le réalisateur du film censé signer le come-back de Frank.

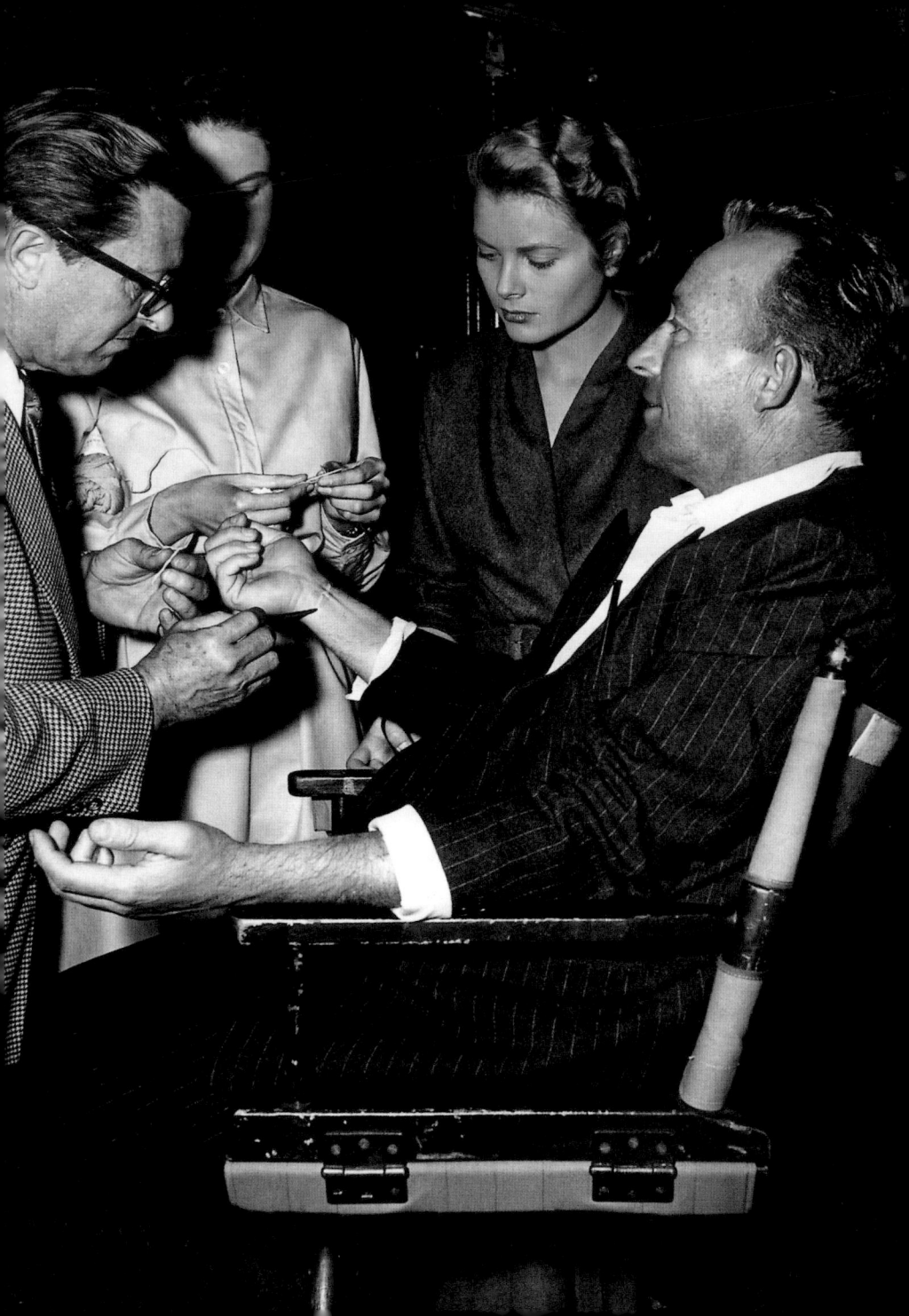

STILL FROM 'THE COUNTRY GIRL' (1954)
Bernie discovers the scars in a shot from the finished
film. / In diesem Bild aus dem fertigen Film entdeckt
Bernie die Narben. / Bernie découvre les plaies do
Frank dans une scène tirée du film une fois celui-ci
achevé.

ON THE SET OF 'THE COUNTRY GIRL' (1954)
Grace watches the makeup of wrist scars being added
to suggest Frank's suicide attempt. / Grace schaut zu,
wie die Maskenbildner Narben auf Bing Crosbys
Handgelenk auftragen, die von Franks versuchtem
Suizid zeugen. / Grace Kelly observe le travail des
maquilleurs sur le poignet de Frank pour la scène de la
tentative de suicide.

STILL FROM 'THE COUNTRY GIRL' (1954)
After Frank's successful return to the stage, Georgie
must decide between Frank and Bernie. / Nach Franks
erfolgreicher Rückkehr ins Rampenlicht muss sich
Georgie zwischen Frank und Bernie entscheiden. /
Après le come-back réussi de Frank, Georgie doit
choisir entre ce dernier et Bernie.

STILL FROM 'THE COUNTRY GIRL' (1954)
William Holden recalled that the reception that Grace's
family gave him was "cold and hostile." / William Holden
erinnert sich, dass ihm Grace' Familie „kalt und
feindselig" begegnete. / William Holden se rappelle que
l'accueil réservé par la famille de Grace Kelly avait été
« froid et hostile ».

OSCAR CEREMONY (1955)
At the Oscar ceremony with Bing Crosby, who was nominated for Best Actor. / Während der Oscar-Verleihung mit Bing Crosby, der als bester Schauspieler nominiert war. / Cérémonie des Oscars en compagnie de Bing Crosby, nominé pour le Meilleur acteur.

OSCAR CEREMONY (1955)
Grace on returning to the Bel Air Hotel after winning her Oscar: "Just the two of us ... terrible ... the loneliest moment of my life." / Nachdem sie den Oscar entgegengenommen hatte, kehrte Grace ins Hotel Bel-Air zurück: „Nur wir beide ... schrecklich! Der einsamste Augenblick meines Lebens." / Grace Kelly au moment de regagner l'hôtel Bel Air après avoir remporté un oscar: « Nous deux, tout seuls ... Horrible ... Le plus grand moment de solitude de toute ma vie. »

PAGES 94/95
PORTRAIT (1955)
Screenwriter John Michael Hayes: "I couldn't get over the difference between her personal animation and, if I may say so, her sexuality." / Drehbuchautor John Michael Hayes: „Ich kam nicht über den Unterschied zwischen ihrer persönlichen Lebhaftigkeit und ihrer – wenn ich es mal so ausdrücken darf – Sexualität hinweg." / Le scénariste John Michael Hayes: « Je n'en revenais pas de la différence qu'il y avait entre sa vitalité et, si je puis m'exprimer ainsi, sa sexualité. »

ON THE SET OF 'GREEN FIRE' (1954)
Grace with director Andrew Marton (white cap),
Stewart Granger, Paul Douglas and John Ericson. /
Grace mit Regisseur Andrew Marton (mit der weißen
Mütze), Stewart Granger, Paul Douglas und John
Ericson. / Grace Kelly avec Andrew Marton
(le réalisateur, casquette blanche), Steward Granger,
Paul Douglas et John Ericson.

*"It wasn't pleasant [filming 'Green Fire']. We
worked in a pathetic village – miserable huts and
dirty. Part of the crew got shipwrecked – it was
awful."*
Grace Kelly

STILL FROM 'GREEN FIRE' (1954)
Donald and Catherine Knowland (John Ericson and
Grace Kelly) are siblings who run a coffee plantation. /
Donald und Catherine Knowland (John Ericson und
Grace Kelly) sind Zwillinge, die gemeinsam eine
Kaffeeplantage betreiben. / Les jumeaux Donald et
Catherine Knowland (John Ericson et Grace Kelly)
exploitent une plantation de café.

„[Grünes Feuer] zu drehen war keine angenehme
Erfahrung. Wir arbeiteten in einem erbärmlichen
Dorf, mit Elendshütten und voller Dreck. Ein Teil
der Crew erlitt Schiffbruch – es war schrecklich."
Grace Kelly

« [Le tournage de L'Émeraude tragique] n'a pas été
une partie de plaisir. Nous avons tourné dans un
village miséreux fait de cahutes sordides et
crasseuses. Une partie de l'équipe a fui naufrage,
c'était absolument horrible. »
Grace Kelly

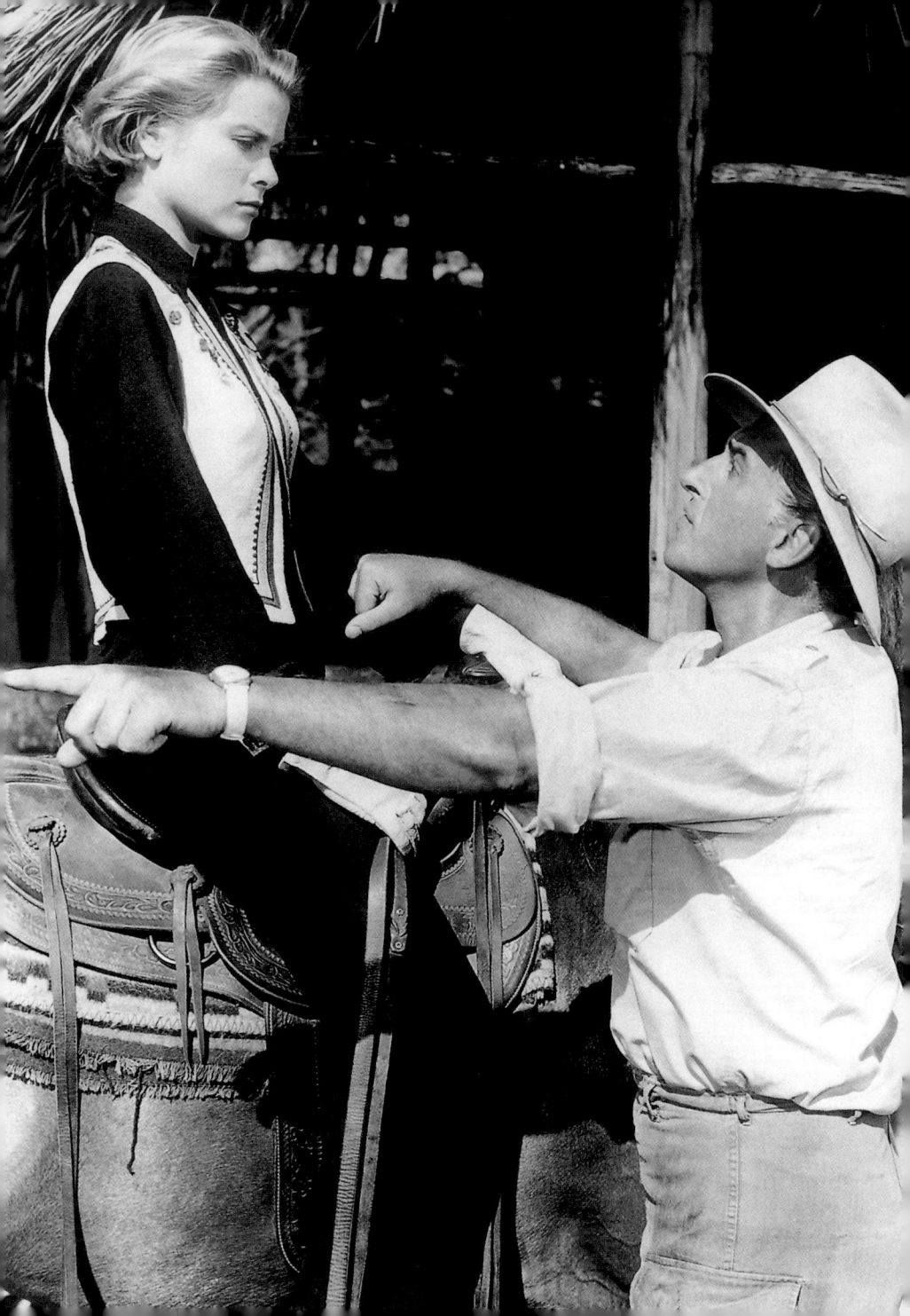

STILL FROM 'GREEN FIRE' (1954)
After the death of her brother, Catherine gets tangled
up in a fight for an emerald mine. / Nach dem Tod ihres
Bruders wird Catherine in den Kampf um eine
Smaragdmine verwickelt. / Après la mort de son frère,
Catherine se voit impliquée dans une lutte sans merci
pour une mine d'émeraude.

STILL FROM 'GREEN FIRE' (1954)
Rian X. Mitchell (Stewart Granger) seeks emeralds in
South America but finds love with Catherine. / Rian X.
Mitchell (Stewart Granger) sucht in Südafrika nach
Smaragden, entdeckt aber stattdessen seine Liebe zu
Catherine. / Parti chercher des émeraudes en
Amérique du Sud, Rian X. Mitchell (Stewart Granger)
y trouve l'amour auprès de Catherine.

STILL FROM 'GREEN FIRE' (1954)
Rian protects Catherine. / Rian beschützt Catherine. /
Rian protège Catherine.

"As an unmarried woman, I was thought to be a
danger. Other women looked on me as a rival,
and it pained me a great deal ... I hated Hollywood.
It's a town without pity."
Grace Kelly

„Als unverheiratete Frau sah man in mir eine
Gefahr. Andere Frauen betrachteten mich als
Rivalin, und das schmerzte mich sehr ... Ich hasste
Hollywood. Es ist eine Stadt, die kein Mitleid
kennt."
Grace Kelly

« Comme je n'étais pas mariée, on voyait en moi un
danger. Les autres femmes me regardaient comme
une rivale, et cela me chagrinait énormément ... Je
détestais Hollywood. C'est une ville sans pitié.»
Grace Kelly

LEFT/LINKS/CI-CONTRE
STILL FROM 'GREEN FIRE' (1954)
Stewart Granger in his autobiography: 'Our last scene
was played in a torrential downpour, and when the final
kiss came we were both soaking wet.' / Stewart Granger
schreibt in seiner Autobiografie: „Unsere letzte Szene
spielte in einem Wolkenbruch. Bei unserem
abschließenden Kuss waren wir beide nass bis auf die
Knochen." / Stewart Granger, dans son autobiographie :
« Notre dernière scène fut jouée sous une pluie
torrentielle et au moment du baiser final, nous étions
tous les deux trempés jusqu'aux os.»

PAGES 104/105
STILL FROM 'GREEN FIRE' (1954)
The film was produced by MGM with whom Grace had
a multi-year contract. / Der Film wurde von MGM
produziert, wo Grace für mehrere Jahre unter Vertrag
stand. / Le film fut produit par la MGM avec laquelle
Grace Kelly avait signé un contrat pluriannuel.

PAGES 106/107
ON THE SET OF 'GREEN FIRE' (1954)
It is regarded today as Grace's least memorable film. /
Der Film gilt heute als Grace' am wenigsten
erinnernswerter Auftritt. / Un rôle considéré
aujourd'hui comme le moins mémorable de Grace Kelly.

POSTER FOR 'GREEN FIRE' (1954)
The advertising stresses the use of color filmstock as much as it touts the stars. / Die Werbung stellte nicht nur die Stars des Films heraus, sondern auch die Tatsache, dass es sich um einen Farbfilm handelte. / Cette publicité vante autant le tournage en couleurs que les vedettes à l'affiche.

PORTRAIT FOR 'GREEN FIRE' (1954)
Actor Alex D'Arcy, one of Grace's romances in New York: "Basically, she was shy. But physically, she was not shy." / Der Schauspieler Alex D'Arcy, mit dem Grace in New York eine kurze Beziehung hatte, meinte: „Im Grunde genommen war Grace schüchtern, aber körperlich war sie überhaupt nicht scheu." / L'acteur Alex D'Arcy, un des amants new-yorkais de Grace Kelly : « Dans le fond, elle était timide. Mais physiquement, elle ne l'était pas. »

STILL FROM 'THE BRIDGES AT TOKO-RI' (1955)
Harry Brubaker (William Holden) on a short furlough
takes his wife Nancy (Grace) and daughters to a
bathhouse. / Während eines kurzen Urlaubs besucht
Harry Brubaker (William Holden) mit seiner Frau Nancy
(Grace) und ihren gemeinsamen Töchtern eine
Badeanstalt. / Profitant d'une permission de courte
durée, Harry Brubaker (William Holden) emmène sa
femme Nancy (Grace Kelly) et ses filles aux thermes.

PAGE 112
STILL FROM 'THE BRIDGES AT TOKO-RI' (1955)
Harry tries to tell Nancy about the dangerous mission
he must fly. / Harry versucht Nancy seine gefährliche
Mission zu erklären. / Harry cherche à s'ouvrir à Nancy à
propos de sa périlleuse mission aérienne.

STILL FROM 'THE BRIDGES AT TOKO-RI' (1955)
Lizanne, Grace's sister: "Bill [Holden] liked Grace an
awful lot ... Whatever quality she had, she should have
bottled it." / Kellys Schwester Lizanne: „Bill [Holden]
hatte Grace sehr gern ... Sie hätte besser ihre Qualitäten, welche auch immer, unter Verschluss halten sol-
len." / Lizanne, la sœur de Grace Kelly : « Bill [Holden]
était follement amoureux de Grace ... Elle aurait mieux
fait de lui cacher ses qualités, quelles qu'elles fussent. »

PAGE 113
STILL FROM 'THE BRIDGES AT TOKO-RI' (1955)
The look of contentment on Nancy's face made this
photo ideal for the film's poster art. / Aufgrund von
Nancys zufriedenem Blick eignete sich dieses Foto
ausgezeichnet für die Plakatwerbung des Films. / Le
visage illuminé de Nancy a fait de ce cliché une affiche
idéale pour le film.

POSTER FOR 'THE BRIDGES AT TOKO-RI' (1955)

The art and billing exploit Grace's growing popularity, making her small part seem more than it is. / Das Filmposter schlägt aus Grace Kellys wachsender Popularität Kapital und lässt ihre Rolle bedeutender erscheinen, als sie es tatsächlich ist. / Tête d'affiche pour rôle secondaire : les affichistes ont su exploiter la popularité grandissante de Grace Kelly.

PAGES 116–119
ARTICLE IN 'MOTION PICTURE' (NOVEMBER 1955)

A contemporary magazine article on Grace's background complete with pictures of her life in Philadelphia. / Ein zeilgenössischer Zeitschriftenartikel über Grace Kellys Herkunft, mit Bildern aus ihrem Leben in Philadelphia. / Article tiré d'un magazine contemporain sur le passé de Grace Kelly, abondamment illustré de photos de ses années de jeunesse à Philadelphie.

ON THE SET OF 'THE BRIDGES AT TOKO-RI' (1955)

It is in bed that Nancy insists on being told about the bridges Harry must attack. / Im Bett besteht Nancy darauf, dass Harry ihr von den Brücken erzählt, die er aus der Luft angreifen soll. / C'est dans le lit conjugal que Nancy exige de Harry qu'il lui parle des ponts qu'il doit attaquer.

Home town report on

Grace Kelly

By Patty de Roulf

A lovely face, the grace and charm of a goddess, an innate sense of what it takes to be a star—this is Grace Kelly today. But it wasn't always so, as writer Patty de Roulf found out when she trekked to Philadelphia to talk with Grace's family, her friends, her neighbors. As these people spoke of the Grace they knew, Miss de Roulf found that not one picture of La Kelly, but many emerged. Like most of us, Grace went through all of those wonderful, wacky and oh-so-normal stages of growing up—the heartaches, the tears and, best of all, the intense joys of adolescence. Here, then, is how it happened.

Henry Avenue mansion, Grace's family home in Philadelphia.

A beribboned, slightly knock-kneed and whiny-voiced Grace Kelly looked at her best friend, Alice Waters, and declared, "Let's do it!"

Grace and Alice, aged eight and ten, had just seen a movie about Madame Curie, and they decided, between giggles, to set up a chemical lab in Alice's basement. After collecting and arranging bottles of colored water on an improvised table, Grace and Alice lured a neighboring youngster named Rusty Koelle down to their lab, ceremonially poured green water into a glass of diluted milk, and turned to the wide-eyed Rusty.

"Now," declared Grace in Dracula-like tones, "we are about to blow you up!" Whereupon she dashed seltzer water into the concoction for added dramatic effect.

As the mixture fizzed and popped, Rusty screamed blue murder and fled from the basement. The two little demons hollered with laughter and held their sides while the tears streamed down their cheeks.

"In those days," recalls Alice Waters, "everything was excruciatingly funny to Gracie and me. We attended Ravenhill Academy, a very proper Philadelphia convent, together. It was quite a place. The nuns taught us French from the first grade on, and semiannually we were all cast in Biblical plays. Gracie was usually an angel, but she snickered so much that no one noticed whether or not she had any acting ability."

Friday was their favorite day, and when it arrived, the two girls would trot over to Alice's house after school, get down the *Boston Cookbook*, search for a recipe which called for few ingredients and set to work. Invariably they wound up making vinegar candy, and at dinner time, Grace would walk around the corner to her own house, carrying a large bowl of her culinary creation and insist that the members of her family sample same.

"Gracie's father was running for mayor of Philadelphia at the time," remembers Alice. "And my dad also was

1937: Mrs. Kelly, Lizanne, Grace (aged 7), and Peggy attend fashion show at Penn Athletic Club.

1950: Kelly anniversary: front row, Grace, Mom, Dad, Peggy. Standing, Kell, Lizanne and friend.

This is Grace's favorite picture of her father, taken on Florida vacation. He cut in at the country club dance.

in city politics. I'm afraid Gracie and I were the bane of their existence. Though we lived half a block from each other, we had long phone conversations every evening. Our poor fathers never could get on the line. One of them would have to go to the other's home to carry on a conversation."

According to Alice, Grace Kelly was possessed of a most vivid imagination. When she was 12, Grace was a Pink Girl, a wartime hospital volunteer. Her job was to carry food trays to patients. On one occasion, she brought in a meal to a man whose eyes were bandaged. Grace not only offered to feed the patient, but decided to add zest to the repast.

"You are now tasting rare green turtle soup, imported directly from the king's palace in Barcelona," she told the poor fellow as she spooned out a thin, tasteless broth. A lowly

veal chop was described by Grace in equally glowing terms, and when it came to dessert, Grace was equal to the occasion. "And now," she said, "two waiters are lighting the brandy on your crêpes suzettes. My, how the flame glows! Now they are dipping them out of the gleaming chafing dish. Gee, it smells divine!" Thus she made tapioca pudding sound wonderful.

Another of Grace's Ravenhill pals was Dottie Langdon, who recalls Grace Kelly had almost platinum blonde hair when she was five, but that it grew darker as she got older.

"She was always quiet-spoken, very feminine and sensitive," says Dottie. "She would cry at the drop of a hat. I don't mean that she was a cry baby. It was just that she felt things deeply. The Kellys had two huge boxers named Wrinkles and Siegfried. Once, Siegfried was sick and had to be taken to the vet. When Grace described his

condition to her friends, she bawled like a baby."

Dottie remembers Grace was good at French and that she would sing French folk tunes at parties "in a sweet voice." As a student, Dottie says Grace was above average, but didn't like the sciences or math. All the girls at Ravenhill were taught to write in a printing style, a script which Grace still uses.

"She was a giver," Dottie relates. "In games, she'd say, 'You go first.' When she was very young, she was painfully shy and often drew within herself. I always thought she had a lovely spiritual quality."

The person who remembers more about Grace Kelly than anybody is her mother, Mrs. Margaret Kelly, who gave birth to the seven-and-a-half pound baby girl at Philadelphia's Hahnemann Hospital on November 12, 1929.

1932: Howard Wikoff, with Grace (aged 2½), who knew her as a baby, says she was a pouter.

1946. Grace attended spring house party with Jack Oechsle, whom she frequently dated. It was cold that week end.

Today, Howard Wikoff and his wife still see Grace on her frequent visits to Philadelphia.

1948: Grace and Jack Oechsle tried out the "kissing ring" at engagement party of his sister, Jean, Grace's best pal.

"Grace was an obedient baby," says Mrs. Kelly, looking back through the years. "She loved attention, but she didn't cry if she didn't get it."

Grace was raised in a big, red brick house on Henry Avenue She was the third offspring of Mr. and Mrs. John B. Kelly, preceded by Peggy and John, Jr., and followed by sister Lizanne. She was the most delicate of the four children, frequently catching cold and suffering from sinus which left a nasal voice that she later overcame. "She loved buttered bread with sugar on it," recalls Mrs. Kelly, "and she hated red cabbage. Like her sisters, Grace collected dolls, but somehow she managed to play with Peggy's and Lizanne's dolls and keep her own in brand-new condition."

Grace Kelly was always a hoarder. She saved everything—letters, programs, badges, snapshots and old clothes. Also, [Please turn to page 67]

Godfrey Ford

Alice Waters

Dottie Langdon

Jean Oechsle

Tommy Schribener

Thomas Keon

STILL FROM 'TO CATCH A THIEF' (1955)
Cary Grant: "Grace acted the way Johnny Weissmuller swam or Fred Astaire danced. She made it look so easy." / Cary Grant: „Grace schauspielerte so, wie Johnny Weissmüller schwamm oder Fred Astaire tanzte. Bei ihr sah es ganz leicht aus." / Cary Grant: «Grace jouait comme Johnny Weissmuller nageait et Fred Astaire dansait. Avec elle, tout avait l'air facile.»

ON THE SET OF 'TO CATCH A THIEF' (1955)
Cary Grant and Grace Kelly get acquainted for this publicity photo. / Cary Grant und Grace Kelly rücken für dieses Werbefoto zusammen. / Cary Grant et Grace Kelly se rapprochent à l'occasion d'une séance de photos publicitaires.

ON THE SET OF 'TO CATCH A THIEF' (1955)
Alfred Hitchcock gives directions in the blistering heat, but Grace remains cool. / Trotz der Gluthitze nimmt Grace Alfred Hitchcocks Regieanweisungen kühl entgegen. / Alfred Hitchcock, qui dirige le tournage, souffre de la chaleur écrasante ; Grace Kelly, quant à elle, reste fraîche comme une rose.

STILL FROM 'TO CATCH A THIEF' (1955)
Grace and Cary Grant became lifelong friends after working on the film. / Nach ihrer gemeinsamen Arbeit an diesem Film wurden Grace Kelly und Cary Grant Freunde fürs Leben. / Après le tournage du film, Grace Kelly et Cary Grant se lieront d'une amitié qui durera jusqu'à la mort de l'actrice.

PAGES 124/125
ON THE SET OF 'TO CATCH A THIEF' (1955)
The first shot of her in the film – as Frances Stevens on the beach at Cannes. / Ihr erster Auftritt in *Über den Dächern von Nizza* – als Frances Stevens am Strand von Cannes. / La scène de *La Main au collet* où Grace apparaît pour la première fois – dans le rôle de Frances Stevens sur la plage de Cannes.

STILL FROM 'TO CATCH A THIEF' (1955)
Ex-cat burglar John Robie (Cary Grant) receives an
audacious, unexpected kiss at the hotel door. / Der
ehemalige Fassadenkletterer John Robie (Cary Grant)
erhält an der Hoteltür einen kühnen und unerwarteten
Kuss. / L'ex-cambrioleur John Robie, dit « Le Chat », est
gratifié d'un baiser inattendu et audacieux devant la
chambre d'hôtel de Frances.

STILL FROM 'TO CATCH A THIEF' (1955)
Princess Stéphanie: "There was so much magic that
surrounded Mom. She almost stopped being human." /
Prinzessin Stéphanie: „Mama war von einem solchen
Zauber umgeben, dass sie schon fast kein Mensch mehr
war." / La princesse Stéphanie : « Il y avait un tel halo de
magie autour de maman. Elle avait presque arrêté d'être
un être humain. »

STILL FROM 'TO CATCH A THIEF' (1955)
Biographer James Spada wrote that: 'Grace joked that
her driving "caused Cary Grant to turn dead white
under his tan."' / Der Biograf James Spada schrieb:
„Grace witzelte, dass Cary Grant bei ihrem Fahrstil
‚unter seiner Sonnenbräune kreidebleich' geworden
sei." / James Spada, biographe de Grace Kelly : « Grace
faisait remarquer en plaisantant que lorsqu'elle prenait
le volant, "Cary Grant devenait blanc comme un linge
sous son bronzage". »

STILL FROM 'TO CATCH A THIEF' (1955)
Frances Stevens: "Would you like a leg or a breast?"
John Robie: "You make the choice." /
Frances Stevens: „Wollen Sie Keule oder Brust?"
John Robie: „Das überlass ich Ihnen." /
Frances Stevens: « Vous voulez l'aile ou le pilon ? »
John Robie: « Faites votre choix. »

ON THE SET OF 'TO CATCH A THIEF' (1955)

Hitchcock's assistant Herbert Coleman: "She wasn't the slightest bit temperamental." / Hitchcocks Assistent Herbert Coleman: „Sie war überhaupt nicht launenhaft." / l lorbert Coleman, l'assistant de Hitchcock: « Elle n'était pas le moins du monde lunatique. »

STILL FROM 'TO CATCH A THIEF' (1955)

Screenwriter John Michael Hayes: "I spent a week with Grace and got to know that she was whimsical ... and teasing." / Drehbuchautor John Michael Hayes: „Ich verbrachte eine Woche mit Grace und stellte dabei fest, dass sie humorvoll war ... und neckisch." / Le scénariste John Michael Hayes: « J'ai passé une semaine avec Grace et j'ai pu découvrir son côté fantasque ... et taquin. »

PAGES 132 & 133

ON THE SET OF 'TO CATCH A THIEF' (1955)

Hitchcock biographer Patrick McGilligan: 'The stunning actress worked and played hard, both virtues the director admired.' Screenwriter John Michael Hayes: "She was like the girl next door, but she was very sexy." / Hitchcock-Biograf Patrick McGilligan: „Die überwältigende Schauspielerin war ebenso hart in der Arbeit wie im Spiel, und der Regisseur bewunderte beide Tugenden." Drehbuchautor John Michael Hayes: „Sie war wie das Mädchen von nebenan, aber sie war sehr sexy." / Patrick McGilligan, biographe d'Alfred Hitchcock: « C'était une fille époustouflante qui travaillait beaucoup et qui jouait ses rôles à fond, deux qualités que le réalisateur admirait chez elle. » Le scénariste John Michael Hayes: « C'était une fille comme les autres, mais elle était tellement sexy. »

STILL FROM 'TO CATCH A THIEF' (1955)
Frances Stevens: "I have a feeling that tonight you're
going to see one of the Riviera's most fascinating
sights." / Frances Stevens: „Ich habe das Gefühl,
Sie erleben heute Nacht noch eine der größten
Sehenswürdigkeiten der Riviera." / Frances Stevens:
« J'ai l'impression que vous assisterez ce soir au
spectacle le plus fascinant qui soit. »

STILL FROM 'TO CATCH A THIEF' (1955)
Frances Stevens: "I was talking about the fireworks!"
John Robie: "I never doubted it." /
Frances Stevens: „Ich spreche vom Feuerwerk."
John Robie: „Das hab' ich nie bezweifelt." /
Frances Stevens: « Je parle du feu d'artifice! »
John Robie: « Pourquoi préciser? »

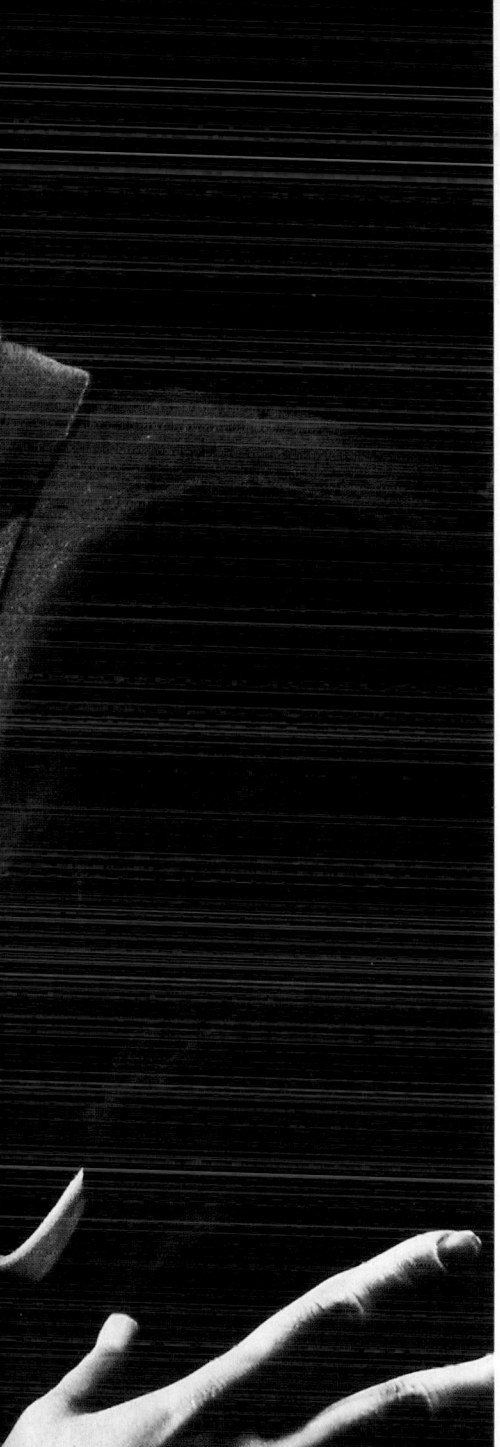

"If you've ever played a love scene with her, you know she's not cold ..."
James Stewart, actor

„Wenn Sie jemals eine Liebesszene mit ihr gespielt haben, dann wissen Sie, dass sie überhaupt nicht kalt ist."
James Stewart, Schauspieler

« Il suffit de jouer une scène d'amour avec elle pour savoir qu'elle n'est pas froide ... »
James Stewart, acteur

STILL FROM 'TO CATCH A THIEF' (1955)
The romantic passion is intercut with shots of the fireworks display. / Die leidenschaftliche Romanze unterbricht Hitchcock mit Aufnahmen explodierender Feuerwerkskörper. / Les scènes de passion romantique sont entrecoupées de tirs de feux d'artifice.

ON THE SET OF 'TO CATCH A THIEF' (1955)
The crew look on intently. / Die Crew schaute gespannt
zu. / L'équipe observe la scène avec intérêt.

"[Hitchcock] would have used Grace in the next
ten pictures he made. I would say that all the
actresses he cast subsequently were attempts to
retrieve the image and feeling that Hitch carried
around so reverentially about Grace."
John Michael Hayes, screenwriter

„[Hitchcock] hätte Grace noch in seinen nächsten
zehn Filmen besetzt. Ich glaube, dass all die
Schauspielerinnen, die er nach ihr für die Rollen
wählte, nur Versuche waren, das Bild von Grace
und die Gefühle wieder zum Leben zu erwecken,
die Hitch so ehrfürchtig mit sich herumtrug."
John Michael Hayes, Drehbuchautor

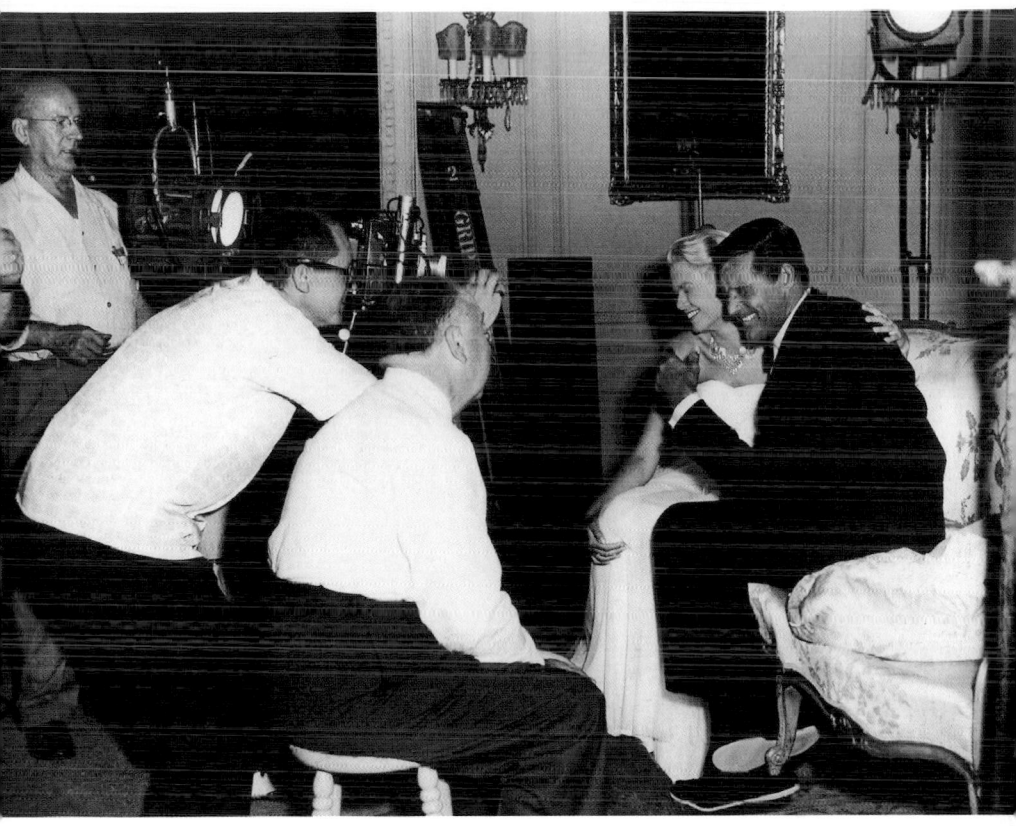

ON THE SET OF 'TO CATCH A THIEF' (1955)
Hitchcock breaks the tension with a well-chosen quip. /
Mit einem wohlüberlegten Scherz löst Hitchcock die
Spannung. / Hitchcock lance une boutade fort à propos
pour détendre l'atmosphère.

*« [Hitchcock] aurait fait jouer Grace dans ses dix
prochains films. Je dirais que toutes les actrices
qu'il a été amené à auditionner par la suite n'ont
été que des tentatives visant à retrouver l'image et
les impressions qu'il avait si humblement
conservées de Grace. »*
John Michael Hayes, scénariste

STILL FROM 'TO CATCH A THIEF' (1955)
The film's finale occurs at a costume ball. / Das Finale
des Films spielt auf einem Kostümball. / La fin du film a
pour cadre un bal costumé.

ON THE SET OF 'TO CATCH A THIEF' (1955)
Edith Head referred to the film as a "costume designer's
dream." / Edith Head nannte den Film den „Traum eines
Kostümbildners". / Edith Head a parlé du film comme
d'un « rêve de costumier ».

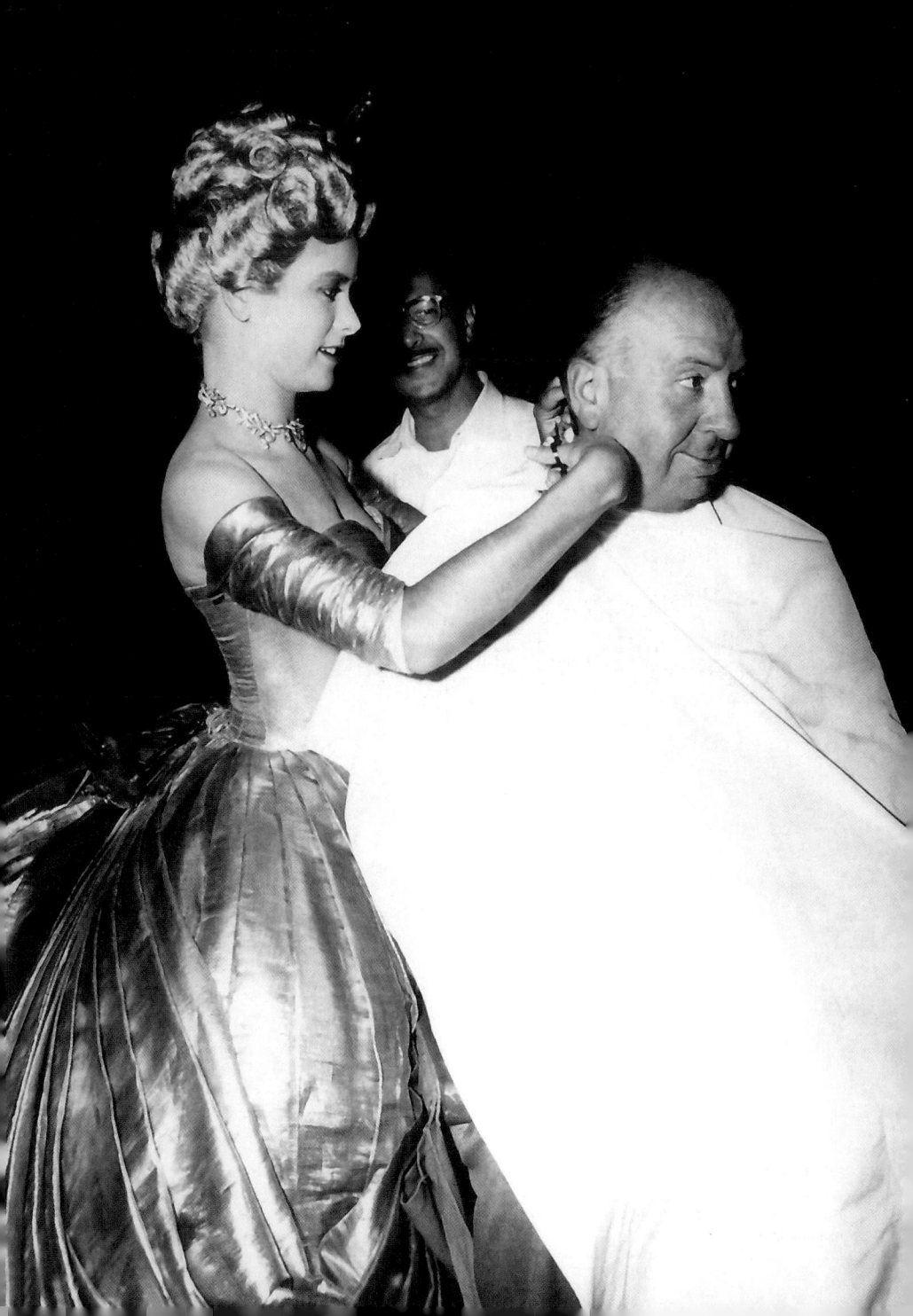

ON THE SET OF 'TO CATCH A THIEF' (1955)

ON THE SET OF 'TO CATCH A THIEF' (1955)
A haircut from Grace. / Grace schneidet Hitch die
Haare. / Hitchcock a droit à une coupe de cheveux des
mains mêmes de Grace Kelly.

STILL FROM 'TO CATCH A THIEF' (1955)
Watching the danger on the rooftop from the terrace below. / Von der Terrasse aus beobachten die Ballgäste ängstlich, was sich auf dem Dach abspielt. / Les invités observent la scène avec angoisse depuis la terrasse.

PAGES 146/147
STILL FROM 'TO CATCH A THIEF' (1955)
The final scene in which John Robie (Cary Grant) gets a wife, and a mother-in-law. / In der Schlussszene findet John Robie (Cary Grant) nicht nur eine Ehefrau, sondern auch eine Schwiegermutter. / Dans la scène de clôture, John Robie (Cary Grant) trouve non seulement une épouse, mais aussi une belle-mère.

ON THE SET OF 'TO CATCH A THIEF' (1955)
The rooftop finale in which the real thief is revealed. / Beim großen Showdown über den Dächern von Nizza wird der wahre Dieb überführt. / La scène finale sur le toit révèle la véritable identité du cambrioleur.

POSTER FOR 'THE SWAN' (1956)
It was the only time in her career that Grace received
top billing. / Dies war der einzige Film in ihrer Karriere,
bei dem Grace an erster Stelle genannt wurde. / Grace
Kelly tient le haut de l'affiche ... pour la première et
dernière fois de sa carrière.

STILL FROM 'THE SWAN' (1956)
Location shooting took place at the Biltmore Estate in
Asheville, North Carolina. / Die Außenaufnahmen
fanden auf Gut Biltmore bei Asheville in North Carolina
statt. / Le château de Biltmore à Asheville, en Caroline
du Nord, a servi de lieu de tournage pour les scènes en
décors naturels.

STILL FROM 'THE SWAN' (1956)
Grace and Alec Guinness won each other's respect and
friendship. / Grace und Alec Guinness lernten sich
kennen und schätzen. / Grace Kelly et Alec Guinness se
vouent un respect et une amitié réciproques.

STILL FROM 'THE SWAN' (1956)
The film is based on a play by Ferenc Molnár; Grace had
played the part on television on 9 June 1950. / Der Film
basiert auf dem Theaterstück *A hattyú* (*Der Schwan*)
von Ferenc Molnár. Grace hatte die Rolle bereits am
9. Juni 1950 im Fernsehen gespielt. / *Le Cygne* est tiré
d'une pièce de Ferenc Molnár. Grace Kelly avait
interprété le même rôle dans un téléfilm diffusé 6 ans
plus tôt, le 9 juin 1950.

STILL FROM 'THE SWAN' (1956)

STILL FROM 'THE SWAN' (1956)

Louis Jourdan: "She had this extraordinary sense of humor ... first of all, about herself, never taking herself seriously." / Louis Jourdan: „Sie besaß einen außergewöhnlichen Sinn für Humor ... vor allem, was sie selbst anging: Sie nahm sich nie ernst." / Louis Jourdan: « Elle avait un sens de l'humour extraordinaire ... surtout lorsqu'elle parlait de sa propre personne ; elle ne se prenait pas au sérieux. »

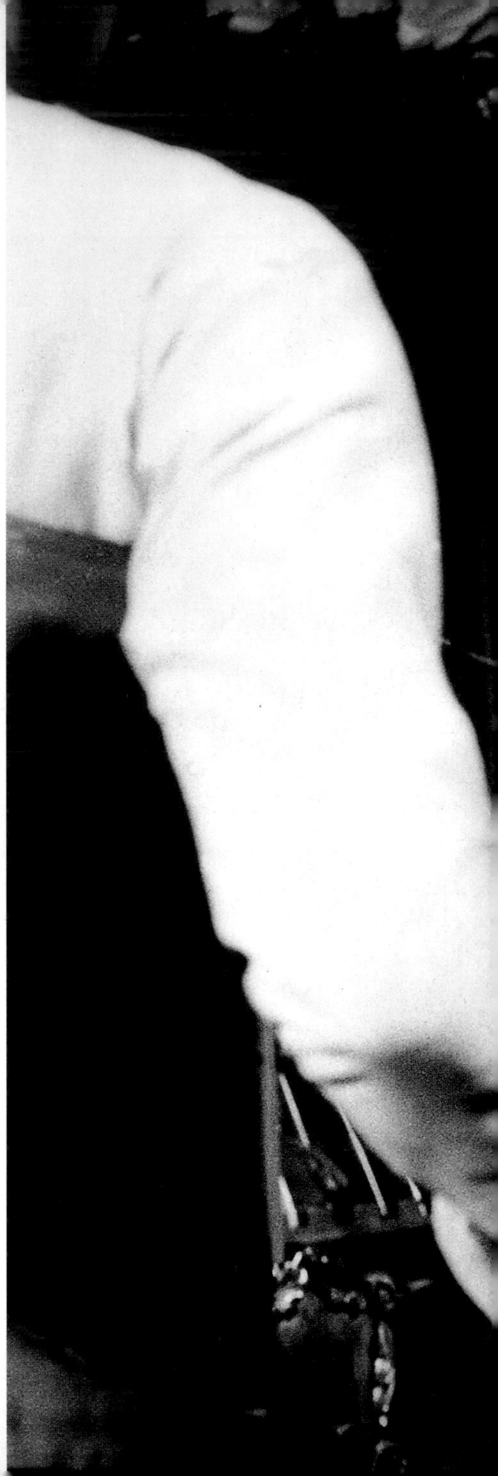

RIGHT/RECHTS/CI-CONTRE
STILL FROM 'THE SWAN' (1956)
Grace learned to do her own fencing for the film and
would not use a double. / Grace lehnte es ab, gedoubelt
zu werden, und lernte für den Film fechten. / Grace
Kelly ne souhaitait pas être doublée et a appris à manier
l'épée pour les besoins du film.

PAGES 156/157
STILL FROM 'THE SWAN' (1956)
Biographer Robert Lacey: 'Offered the choice between
a life of passion and ... position, the heroine opts for
status.' / Biograf Robert Lacey: „Vor die Wahl zwischen
Leidenschaft oder Ansehen gestellt, entscheidet sich
die Heldin für den Status." / Robert Lacey, biographe
de Grace Kelly : « Entre la passion et ... la réputation,
l'héroïne choisit le statut. »

STILL FROM 'HIGH SOCIETY' (1956)
Grace received a Gold Record for her recording of 'True Love' with Bing Crosby. / Grace erhielt eine Goldene Schallplatte für ihre Aufnahme des Liedes „True Love" mit Bing Crosby. / Grace Kelly a reçu un Disque d'or pour l'enregistrement de la chanson *True Love* en duo avec Bing Crosby.

"I loved acting. I didn't particularly like being a movie star."
Grace Kelly

„Ich liebte die Schauspielerei. Ich mochte es aber nicht besonders, ein Filmstar zu sein."
Grace Kelly

« J'aimais mon métier d'actrice. Mais je n'ai jamais vraiment aimé mon rôle de star de cinéma. »
Grace Kelly

STILL FROM 'HIGH SOCIETY' (1956)
The film is a musical remake of 'The Philadelphia Story'
with songs by Cole Porter. / *Die oberen Zehntausend* ist
ein musikalisches Remake von *Die Nacht vor der
Hochzeit* mit Liedern von Cole Porter. / La comédie
musicale *Haute société* est un remake d'*Indiscrétions*.
Les paroles des chansons sont signées Cole Porter.

PAGES 160/161
ON THE SET OF 'HIGH SOCIETY' (1956)
Photographer Howell Conant: "She had a dancer's
awareness of her body; Grace's arms and legs were as
expressive as her face." / Fotograf Howell Conant: „Sie
besaß das Körperbewusstsein einer Tänzerin. Grace'
Arme und Beine waren ebenso ausdrucksvoll wie ihr
Gesicht." / Le photographe Howell Conant : « Grace
avait une conscience de son corps digne d'une grande
danseuse ; ses bras et ses jambes avaient la même
puissance d'expression que son visage. »

PAGES 162/163
ON THE SET OF 'HIGH SOCIETY' (1956)
Filming with Bing Crosby. / Bei den Dreharbeiten mit
Bing Crosby. / En tournage avec Bing Crosby.

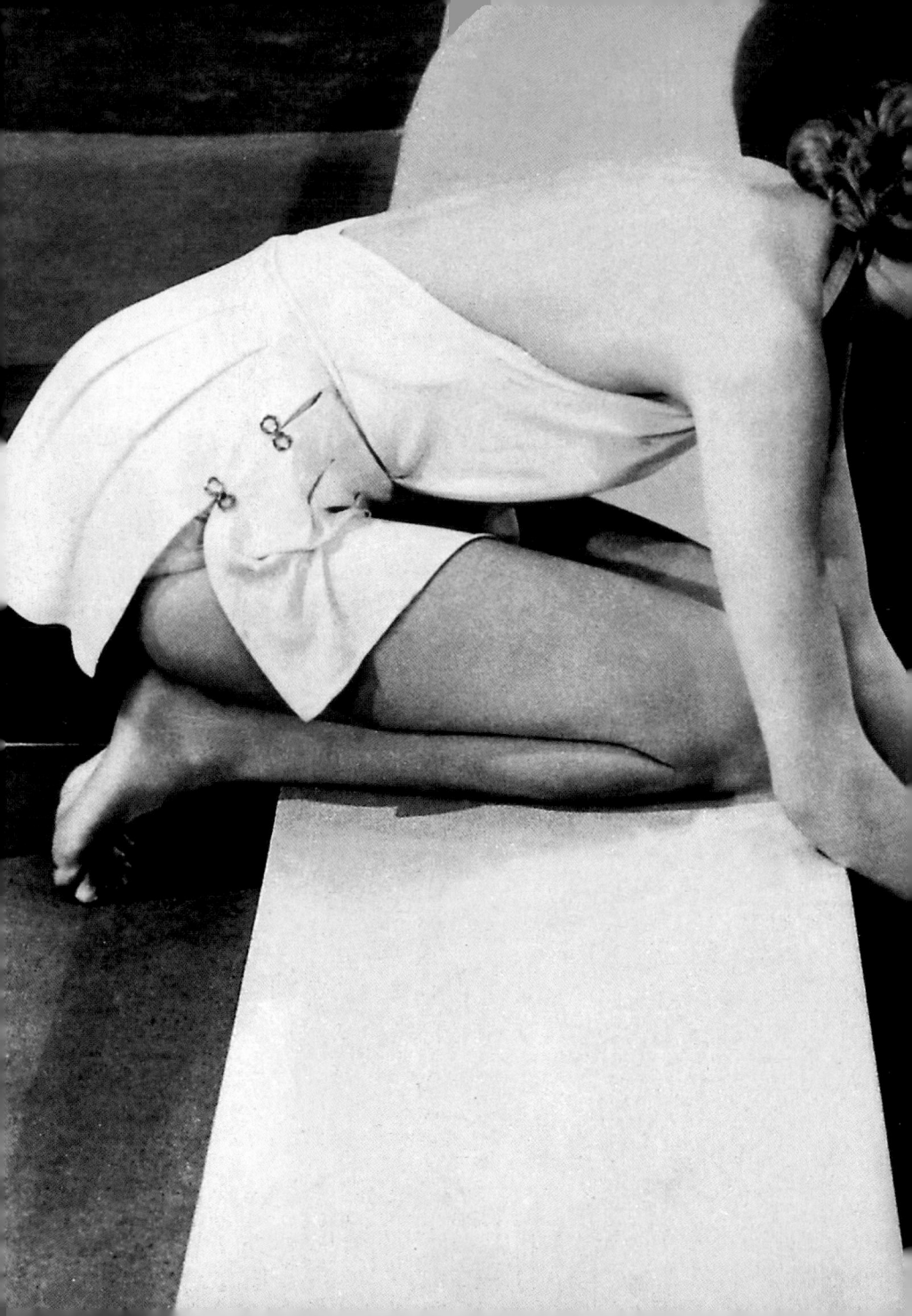

STILL FROM 'HIGH SOCIETY' (1956)
Biographer Robert Lacey: 'For all her frequently expressed ambitions to be a serious actress, Grace seldom took any risks. She knew her limitations.' / Biograf Robert Lacey: „Trotz ihrer unermüdlichen Beteuerungen, eine ernsthafte Schauspielerin werden zu wollen, ging Grace selten Risiken ein. Sie kannte ihre Grenzen." / Robert Lacey, biographe de Grace Kelly: « Si elle manifestait souvent son ambition de devenir une actrice sérieuse, elle évitait le plus souvent de prendre le moindre risque. Elle connaissait ses limites. »

STILL FROM 'HIGH SOCIETY' (1956)
Frank Sinatra plays the magazine reporter with whom Tracy Lord (Grace) has a fling. / Frank Sinatra spielt den Zeitschriftenreporter, mit dem Tracy Lord (Grace) eine Affäre hat. / Frank Sinatra dans le rôle du journaliste de magazine qui entretient une liaison avec Tracy Lord (Grace Kelly).

STILL FROM 'HIGH SOCIETY' (1956)
With John Lund as Tracy's intended. / Mit John Lund als
Tracys Zukünftigem. / En compagnie de John Lund, le
prétendant de Tracy.

PAGES 168/169
ON THE SET OF 'HIGH SOCIETY' (1956)
With director Charles Walters. / Mit Regisseur Charles
Walters. / Aux côtés du réalisateur Charles Walters.

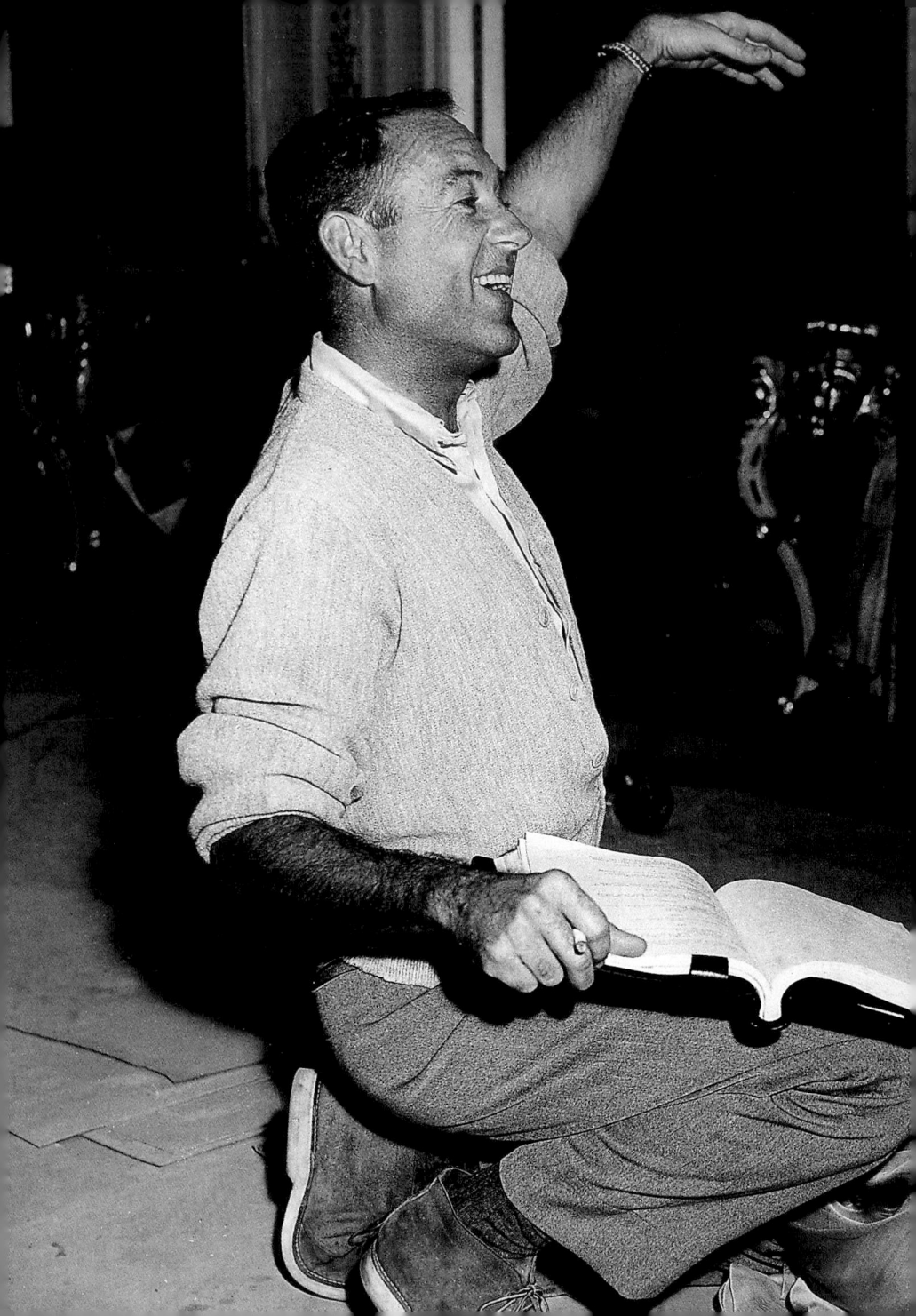

STILL FROM 'HIGH SOCIETY' (1956)
Tracy's tipsy night with Mike Connor (Frank Sinatra). /
Tracys beschwipste Nacht mit Mike Connor (Frank
Sinatra). / La soirée bien arrosée de Tracy, en
compagnie de Mike Connor (Frank Sinatra).

STILL FROM 'HIGH SOCIETY' (1956)
Grace and Frank Sinatra and Cole Porter's song 'You're
Sensational.' / Grace Kelly und Frank Sinatra zu Cole
Porters Lied „You're Sensational". / Grace Kelly et Frank
Sinatra interprètent *You're Sensational* de Cole Porter.

"She wasn't just another beautiful girl, she was the essence of freshness."
Fred Coe, director

„Sie war nicht nur irgendein hübsches Mädchen. Sie war die Frische in Person."
Fred Coe, Regisseur

« C'était une femme belle, mais d'une beauté comparable à nulle autre ; elle incarnait la fraîcheur par excellence. »
Fred Coe, réalisateur

STILL FROM 'HIGH SOCIETY' (1956)
And later ... the inevitable explanations. / Und später ... die unvermeidlichen Erklärungen. / Et un peu plus tard ... l'heure des comptes.

ON THE SET OF 'HIGH SOCIETY' (1956)
Ready for the final scene (with the shadow of the
microphone boom visible). / Bereit zur Schlussszene
(am oberen Bildrand ist noch der Schatten des
Galgenmikrofons zu sehen). / Prête pour la scène finale
(l'ombre de la perche est visible dans l'encoignure de la
porte).

PAGES 176/177
STILL FROM 'HIGH SOCIETY' (1956)
The happy ending: Tracy remarries her first husband. /
Ein glückliches Ende: Tracy heiratet wieder ihren ersten
Ehemann. / Happy end! Tracy se remarie avec son
premier époux.

ON THE SET OF 'HIGH SOCIETY' (1956)
With Louis Armstrong. Notice Grace is wearing the
engagement ring given to her by Prince Rainier. / Mit
Louis Armstrong. Man beachte an Grace' Finger den
Verlobungsring, den sie von Fürst Rainier erhielt. / Aux
côtés de Louis Armstrong. Détail intéressant : Grace
Kelly porte au doigt la bague de fiançailles offerte par le
prince Rainier.

COVER FOR 'THE GRACE KELLY STORY'
(1957)

GRACE KELLY MARRIES PRINCE RAINIER
(19 APRIL 1956)

PAGE 180
PORTRAIT (1954)

3
CHRONOLOGY

CHRONOLOGIE

CHRONOLOGIE

CHRONOLOGY

12 November 1929 Born in Philadelphia to John and Margaret Kelly.

1947–1949 Attends the American Academy of Dramatic Arts in New York. Supports herself as a model, appearing on the covers of national magazines *(Redbook, Cosmopolitan)* as well as in magazine ads and, later, television commercials.

1949 July: Theatrical debut at the Bucks County Playhouse in New Hope, Pennsylvania, in *The Torch-Bearers*, a play by her uncle, George Kelly. Also appears with John Carradine in *The Heiress*. November: Broadway debut with Raymond Massey in *The Father* by August Strindberg.

1950–1953 Appears in almost 60 anthology dramas on television.

1951 Screen debut in *Fourteen Hours* in a small part. Performs at the Elitch Gardens Theater in Denver, appearing in ten plays in eleven weeks. In the fall, Grace enrolls in Sanford Meisner's acting class to refine her craft.

1952 Plays Gary Cooper's young bride in *High Noon*. Offered the second female lead in *Mogambo*, to be shot in Africa, if she signs a seven-year contract with MGM.

1953 Academy Award nomination for her role in *Mogambo*. Alfred Hitchcock sees a screen test and casts her in *Dial M for Murder*, the first of their three collaborations.

1954 Stars in four major films: *Dial M for Murder*, *Rear Window* (her second film with Hitchcock), *The Country Girl*, and *Green Fire*. By the end of the year, she is the top female box-office attraction in America. Also films *The Bridges at Toko-Ri* and *To Catch a Thief* (her final Hitchcock film).

1955 30 March: Wins the Academy Award for *The Country Girl* by six votes (according to columnist Hedda Hopper) over Judy Garland in *A Star Is Born*. May: Attends the Cannes Film Festival and meets Prince Rainier of Monaco. Films *The Swan* in America as Rainier commences a long-distance courtship.

1956 5 January: Announces her engagement. Grace appears in *High Society*, her last fiction film, a musical remake of *The Philadelphia Story*. 19 April: Grace and Rainier marry before a television audience of thirty million.

27 January 1957 Gives birth to Princess Caroline.

14 March 1958 Gives birth to Prince Albert.

1962 Accepts Alfred Hitchcock's offer to appear in *Marnie*, but backs out of the project when the citizens of Monaco object.

1 February 1965 Gives birth to Princess Stephanie.

1976–1981 Performs a series of poetry readings in Europe and America.

1977 Performs voice-over and on-camera narration for *The Children of Theatre Street*, an Oscar-nominated documentary about the famous Leningrad (Kirov) ballet school.

1979 Appears as herself in *Rearranged*, a film about Monaco's annual flower-arranging competition.

1980 Participates in an American publicity tour for *My Book of Flowers*, published by Doubleday, a collection of her flower collages previously exhibited in a Paris gallery.

14 September 1982 Dies from injuries sustained the day before in an automobile accident while returning with Princess Stephanie to Monaco from a family retreat.

COVER FOR 'MOTION PICTURE' (NOVEMBER 1955)

Halloween Mischief! Brando, Monroe, Gable go Wild! Wild! Wild!

MOTION PICTURE

MORE FOR

15¢

November

GRACE KELLY

CHRONOLOGIE

12. November 1929 In Philadelphia wird Grace Kelly als Tochter von John und Margaret Kelly geboren.

1947–1949 Sie besucht die American Academy of Dramatic Arts in New York. Ihren Lebensunterhalt verdient sie als Fotomodell und ist sowohl auf den Titelbildern landesweit vertriebener Zeitschriften (Redbook, Cosmopolitan) als auch in Zeitschriftenanzeigen und später in Fernsehwerbespots zu sehen.

1949 Juli: Theaterdebüt im Bucks County Playhouse in New Hope (Pennsylvania) in The Torch-Bearers, einem Stück aus der Feder ihres Onkels George Kelly. Außerdem steht sie mit John Carradine in The Heiress auf der Bühne. November: Broadway-Debüt mit Raymond Massey in Fadren (Der Vater) von August Strindberg.

1950–1953 Knapp 60 TV-Auftritte in Serien und Fernsehspielen.

1951 Leinwanddebüt in Vierzehn Stunden in einer kleinen Rolle. Innerhalb von elf Wochen tritt sie in zehn Bühnenstücken am Elitch Gardens Theater in Denver (Colorado) auf. Im Herbst schreibt sich Grace an der Schauspielschule von Sanford Meisner ein, um ihre Kunst weiter zu verbessern.

1952 Sie spielt die frischvermählte Ehefrau des Marshalls (Gary Cooper) in 12 Uhr mittags. Außerdem bietet man ihr im Gegenzug für einen Siebenjahresvertrag mit MGM die zweite weibliche Hauptrolle in Mogambo an, der in Afrika gedreht werden soll.

1953 Für ihre Rolle in Mogambo wird sie für den Academy Award (Oscar) nominiert. Alfred Hitchcock sieht eine Kameraprobe und gibt ihr eine Rolle in Bei Anruf Mord, dem ersten ihrer drei gemeinsamen Filme.

1954 Sie spielt die Hauptrolle in vier großen Filmen: Bei Anruf Mord, Das Fenster zum Hof, ihrem zweiten Film mit Hitchcock, Ein Mädchen vom Lande und Grünes Feuer. Am Jahresende ist sie in den USA der weibliche Star, der die höchsten Einspielergebnisse erzielt. Sie dreht außerdem Die Brücken von Toko-Ri und Über den Dächern von Nizza, ihren letzten Hitchcock-Film.

PORTRAIT (1954)

1955 30. März: Sie erhält einen Academy Award (Oscar) für Ein Mädchen vom Lande – der Kolumnistin Hedda Hopper zufolge mit einem Vorsprung von sechs Stimmen vor Judy Garland in Ein neuer Stern am Himmel. Mai: Sie besucht das Filmfestival in Cannes und lernt dort Fürst Rainier von Monaco kennen. Sie dreht Der Schwan in Amerika, während Fürst Rainier beginnt, aus der Ferne um sie zu werben.

1956 5. Januar: Das Paar gibt seine Verlobung bekannt. Grace tritt in Die oberen Zehntausend, einem Musical-Remake der Komödie Die Nacht vor der Hochzeit, zum letzten Mal in einem Spielfilm auf. 19. April: Die Hochzeit von Grace und Rainier verfolgen 30 Millionen Fernsehzuschauer.

27. Januar 1957 Geburt von Prinzessin Caroline.

14. März 1958 Geburt von Prinz Albert.

1962 Sie nimmt Alfred Hitchcocks Angebot an, die Titelrolle in Marnie zu übernehmen, doch auf Druck der Monegassen zieht sie ihre Zusage wieder zurück.

1. Februar 1965 Geburt von Prinzessin Stéphanie.

1976–1981 Sie tritt in Europa und Amerika mit einer Reihe von Dichterlesungen auf.

1977 Sie spricht sowohl vor der Kamera als auch im Voiceover den Kommentar zu dem für einen Oscar nominierten Dokumentarfilm The Children of Theatre Street über die berühmte Kirow-Ballettschule in St. Petersburg.

1979 Sie spielt sich selbst in Rearranged, einem Film über den jährlichen Blumenbindewettbewerb in Monaco.

1980 Sie nimmt an einer Publicity-Tour durch Amerika für die bei Doubleday unter dem Titel My Book of Flowers erschienene Sammlung ihrer Blumencollagen teil, die zuvor in einer Pariser Galerie ausgestellt war.

14. September 1982 Sie erliegt den Folgen ihrer schweren Verletzungen, die sie sich am Vortag bei einem Autounfall zugezogen hatte, als sie mit Prinzessin Stéphanie von der Sommerresidenz der Familie nach Monaco zurückfuhr.

CHRONOLOGIE

12 novembre 1929 Grace naît en 1929 à Philadelphie de John et Margaret Kelly.

1947–1949 Entre à l'American Academy of Dramatic Arts de New York. Gagne sa vie comme mannequin et apparaît en couverture de magazines nationaux *(Redbook, Cosmopolitan)*, ainsi que dans des publicités pour des magazines et, plus tard, pour la télévision.

1949 Juillet : fait ses débuts au théâtre sur les planches du Bucks County Playhouse de New Hope, Pennsylvanie, dans *The Torch-Bearers*, une pièce de son oncle George Kelly. Apparaît également aux côtés de John Carradine dans *L'Héritière*. Novembre : fait ses débuts à Broadway avec Raymond Massey dans *Père* d'August Strindberg.

1950–1953 Apparaît dans près de 60 séries pour la télévision.

1951 Obtient son premier petit rôle à l'écran dans *Quatorze heures*. Se produit au Elitch Gardens Theater de Denver, où elle enchaîne dix pièces pendant onze semaines. S'inscrit, à l'automne, aux cours de théâtre de Sanford Meisner pour se perfectionner.

1952 Joue le rôle de la jeune mariée de Gary Cooper dans *Le train sifflera trois fois*. Se voit proposer le second rôle féminin dans *Mogambo*, dont le tournage doit avoir lieu en Afrique, en échange d'un contrat de sept ans avec la MGM.

1953 Est nominée pour un Academy Award pour son rôle dans *Mogambo*. Alfred Hitchcock visionne un screen-test et auditionne Grace Kelly pour *Le crime était presque parfait*, la première de trois collaborations.

1954 Tient la vedette dans quatre films majeurs : *Le crime était presque parfait, Fenêtre sur cour* (son second film signé Hitchcock), *Une fille de province* et *L'Émeraude tragique*. (À la fin de l'année, elle devient la star numéro un du box-office américain.) Tourne également dans *Les Ponts de Toki-Ri* et *La Main au collet* (son dernier rôle dans un film de Hitchcock).

1955 30 mars : remporte un Academy Award pour *Une fille de province* avec six voix d'avance (selon l'éditorialiste Hedda Hopper) sur Judy Garland pour *Une étoile est née*. Mai : participe au festival de Cannes et rencontre le prince Rainier de Monaco. Tourne dans *Le Cygne* aux États-Unis et entretient avec le prince Rainier une idylle à distance.

1956 5 janvier : annonce ses fiançailles. Apparaît dans la comédie musicale *Haute société*, son dernier film de fiction, remake d'*Indiscrétions* de George Cukor. 19 avril : Grace et le prince Rainier célèbrent leur mariage, suivi par 30 millions de téléspectateurs.

27 janvier 1957 Donne naissance à la princesse Caroline.

14 mars 1958 Donne naissance au prince Albert.

1962 À la demande d'Alfred Hitchcock, accepte un rôle dans *Pas de printemps pour Marnie*, mais finit par décliner la proposition devant la réprobation des citoyens monégasques.

1er février 1965 Donne naissance à la princesse Stéphanie.

1976–1981 Donne des lectures de poésies en Europe et en Amérique.

1977 Prête sa voix pour des doublages et des commentaires de *The Children of Theatre Street*, documentaire consacré à la prestigieuse école de ballet du théâtre Kirov de Leningrad et récompensé par un oscar.

1979 Apparaît dans son propre rôle dans *Rearranged*, documentaire retraçant le concours annuel de compositions florales de Monaco.

1980 Participe à la tournée promotionnelle américaine de *My Book of Flowers*, une collection de ses collages floraux présentée auparavant dans une galerie parisienne.

14 septembre 1982 Grace Kelly décède des suites d'un accident de voiture tandis qu'elle rejoint Monaco avec la princesse Stéphanie après des vacances passées en famille.

COVER FOR 'COLLIER'S' (24 JUNE 1955)

Collier's

JUNE 24, 1955 • FIFTEEN CENTS

TURBOCARS
Detroit Is Working on Your Car of Tomorrow
•
A WIRETAPPER TALKS

On an
Island Vacation
with
GRACE KELLY

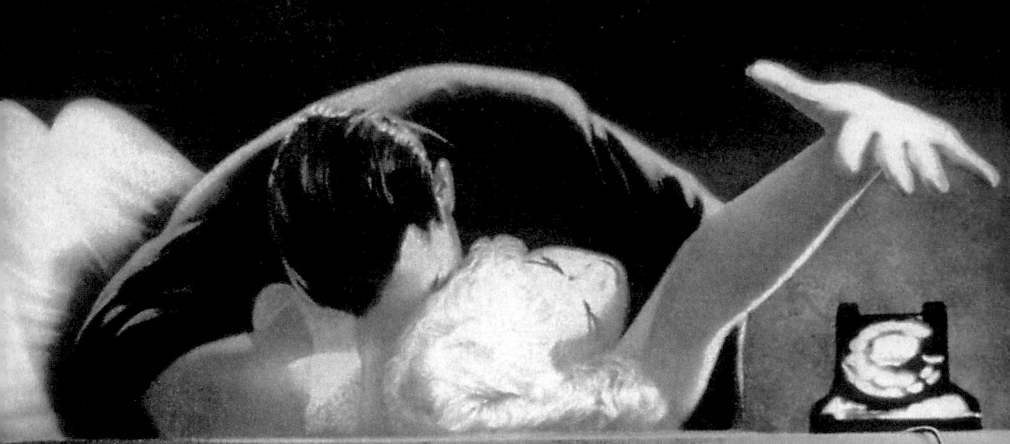

ALFRED
HITCHCOCK'S

"dial
M
for
Murder"

...is that you, darling?"

4

FILMOGRAPHY

FILMOGRAFIE

FILMOGRAPHIE

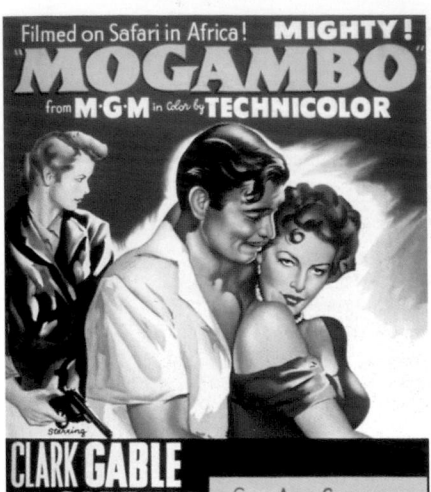

Green Fire (dt. *Grünes Feuer*, fr. *L'Émeraude tragique*, 1954)
Catherine Knowland. Director/Regie/réalisation: Andrew Marton.

The Bridges at Toko-Ri (dt. *Die Brücken von Toko-Ri*, fr. *Les Ponts de Toko-Ri*, 1955)
Nancy Brubaker. Director/Regie/réalisation: Mark Robson.

To Catch a Thief (dt. *Über den Dächern von Nizza*, fr. *La Main au collet*, 1955)
Frances Stevens. Director/Regie/réalisation: Alfred Hitchcock.

The Swan (dt. *Der Schwan*, fr. *Le Cygne*, 1956)
Princess Alexandra/Prinzessin Alexandra/princesse Alexandra. Director/Regie/réalisation: Charles Vidor.

High Society (dt. *Die oberen Zehntausend*, fr. *Haute Société*, 1956)
Tracy Samantha Lord. Director/Regie/réalisation: Charles Waters.

Fourteen Hours (dt. *Vierzehn Stunden*, fr. *Quatorze heures*, 1951)
Mrs. Louise Ann Fuller. Director/Regie/réalisation: Henry Hathaway.

High Noon (dt. *12 Uhr mittags*, fr. *Le train sifflera trois fois*, 1952)
Amy Fowler Kane. Director/Regie/réalisation: Fred Zinnemann.

Mogambo (1953)
Linda Nordley. Director/Regie/réalisation: John Ford.

Dial M for Murder (dt. *Bei Anruf Mord*, fr. *Le crime était presque parfait*, 1954)
Margot Wendice. Director/Regie/réalisation: Alfred Hitchcock.

Rear Window (dt. *Das Fenster zum Hof*, fr. *Fenêtre sur cour*, 1954)
Lisa Carol Fremont. Director/Regie/réalisation: Alfred Hitchcock.

The Country Girl (dt. *Ein Mädchen vom Lande*, fr. *Une fille de province*, 1954)
Georgie Elgin. Director/Regie/réalisation: George Seaton.

The Children of Theatre Street (1977)
Narrator/Erzählerin/narratrice.
Director/Regie/réalisation: Robert Dornhelm.

**Rearranged (1979, no commercial
release/unveröffentlicht/non sorti en salles)**
Herself/Fürstin Gracia Patricia/dans son propre rôle.
Production/Produktion/production: Grace Kelly.
Director/Regie/réalisation: Robert Dornhelm.

BIBLIOGRAPHY

Bradford, Sarah: *Princess Grace.* Stein and Day, 1984.
Conant, Howell: *Grace.* Random House, 1992.
DeRosa, Steven: *Writing with Hitchcock: The Collaboration of Alfred Hitchcock and John Michael Hayes.* Faber and Faber, 2001.
Dherber Yann-Brice & Verlha, Pierre-Henri: *Grace Kelly, les images d'une vie.* Phyb, 2006.
Englund, Steven: *Grace of Monaco.* Doubleday, 1984.
Grace, Princess of Monaco and Gwen Robyns: *My Book of Flowers.* Doubleday, 1980.
Hart-Davis, Phyllida: *Grace: The Story of a Princess.* St. Martin's Press, 1982.
Haugland, Kristina: *Grace: Icon of Style to Royal Bride.* Philadelphia Museum of Art, 2006.
Lacey, Robert: *Grace.* Putnam, 1994.
Leigh, Wendy: *Les Derniers Secrets.* Nouveau Monde, 2007.

Lewis, Arthur H.: *Those Philadelphia Kellys, with a Touch of Grace.* Morrow, 1977.
McGilligan, Patrick: *Alfred Hitchcock: A Life in Darkness and Light.* Regan Books, 2003.
Quine, Judith Balaban: *The Bridesmaids: Grace Kelly and Six Intimate Friends.* Simon and Schuster, 1989.
Robinson, Jeffrey: *Rainier and Grace: An Intimate Portrait.* Atlantic Monthly Press, 1989.
Robyns, Gwen: *Princess Grace.* McKay, 1976.
Spada, James: *Grace: The Secret Lives of a Princess.* Doubleday, 1987.
Taraborrelli, J. Randy: *Once Upon a Time: Behind the Fairy Tale of Princess Grace and Prince Rainier.* Warner Books, 2003.
Tierney, Tom: *Grace Kelly: Paper Dolls in Full Color.* Dover, 1986.
Wayne, Jane Ellen: *Grace Kelly's Men.* St. Martin's Press, 1991.
Weber, Patrick: *Monaco, la saga Grimaldi.* Timée-Éditions, 2007.

P-170

IMPRINT

© 2007 TASCHEN GmbH
Hohenzollernring 53, D-50672 Köln
www.taschen.com

Editor/Picture Research/Layout: Paul Duncan/Wordsmith Solutions
Editorial Coordination: Martin Holz, Cologne
Production Coordination: Nadia Najm and Horst Neuzner, Cologne
German Translation: Thomas J. Kinne, Nauheim
French Translation: Arnaud Briand, Paris
Multilingual production: www.arnaudbriand.com, Paris
Typeface Design: Sense/Net, Andy Disl and Birgit Reber, Cologne

Printed in Italy
ISBN 978-3-8228-2221-0

To stay informed about upcoming TASCHEN titles, please request our magazine at www.taschen.com/magazine or write to TASCHEN, Hohenzollernring 53, D-50672 Cologne, Germany, contact@taschen.com, Fax: +49-221-254919. We will be happy to send you a free copy of our magazine which is filled with information about all of our books.

All the photos in this book, except for those listed below, were supplied by The Kobal Collection.
British Film Institute Stills, Posters and Designs, London: pp. 2/3, 6/7, 26/27, 28, 30, 31, 35, 44, 45, 48, 50/51, 58, 63, 64, 71, 82, 86/87, 91, 98, 99, 109, 113, 115, 133, 143, 149, 162/163, 190ll. Thanks to Dave Kent, Phil Moad and everybody at The Kobal Collection for their professionalism and kindness.